IGNITION AND TIMING

A GUIDE TO REBUILDING, REPAIR AND REPLACEMENT

IGNITION AND TIMING

A GUIDE TO REBUILDING, REPAIR AND REPLACEMENT

Colin Beever

THE CROWOOD PRESS

First published in 2015 by
The Crowood Press Ltd
Ramsbury, Marlborough
Wiltshire SN8 2HR

www.crowood.com

British Library Cataloguing-in-Publication Data
A catalogue record for this book is available from the British Library.

ISBN 978 1 84797 973 5

Disclaimer
Safety is of the utmost importance in every aspect of an automotive
workshop. The practical procedures and the tools and equipment used
in automotive workshops are potentially dangerous. Tools should be
used in strict accordance with the manufacturer's recommended
procedures and current health and safety regulations. The author
and publisher cannot accept responsibility for any accident or
injury caused by following the advice given in this book.

Typeset by Servis Filmsetting Ltd, Stockport, Cheshire
Printed and bound in India by Replika Press Pvt Ltd

CONTENTS

ACKNOWLEDGEMENTS

I would like to thank the following people for their kind help in providing information and images for use in this book: Tim Ward of Lucas TRW; the Marketing Department of NGK Spark Plugs (UK) Ltd; Tom Green of the Green Spark Plug Company; Steve Pearce of Autocar Electrical Equipment Co. Ltd; and Keith Anderson of The Tool Connection Ltd.

INTRODUCTION

Everybody running or restoring a classic car will at some point have ignition problems. These need to be corrected properly and with the appropriate components in order to prolong the car's life and increase its running efficiency. A distributor is at the heart of the car's engine system, and yet so often it is overlooked.

This book looks at the history and evolution of the automotive ignition system, from the very basic early distributor and coil ignition up to the introduction of electronic ignition. It covers both manufacturer-fitted and aftermarket ignition systems, and considers the demise of the points-type distributor and the introduction of electronic ignition. It will also provide you with an understanding of how the coil ignition system works, looking at each of the components and explaining how to test them for faults, and then how to rectify these faults.

Whether you are just changing a set of points, attempting your own rebuild, or modifying your car for competition, you will find tips and advice as to how to put your ignition in top spec. The first chapter looks at the history of the ignition system, and shows its development over the years. Then the technical side of ignition is discussed, and simple tests given to identify a problem and then show how to rectify it.

Later in the book we look at modifying the system, fitting various types of electronic ignition, and modifying the distributor in order to achieve maximum performance.

In the last section identification charts are provided: these are both informative and useful, as many classic cars will have had their distributors changed at some point in their life; this section shows you how to find out if you have the correct one fitted.

The following tools may be required for maintaining early ignition systems:

- Points file, such as the Draper 33554
- Timing light – the Gunson Supastrobe G4123 is a great unit

- Multimeter – the Gunson G4187
- Insulated screwdrivers, both flat-head and cross-head
- Feeler gauge – both metric and imperial would be useful
- Spanners – choose the size that fits the distributor clamp: this may vary

Make sure that the car's battery is in good condition and fully charged. Check it with a volt meter; ideally you should be getting about 12.5 volts from a good battery.

When working on distributors that have been removed from the vehicle, make sure that they are firmly secured in a bench vice – though always remember that too much pressure can cause damage. Make sure that all surfaces are clean and free from dust, as this can cause contamination and damage. All tools should be in good condition, as worn screwdrivers and spanners can easily cause damage.

HEALTH AND SAFETY WARNINGS

When working on vehicle ignition systems you must always put the safety of both yourself and others first. The publishers and author of this book cannot accept any responsibility for injury or damage when following instructions or carrying out work as described in this book.

Never carry out work on live systems, and always disconnect the battery as advised; also, remember that you must always remove the earth terminal first, but reconnect it last – this is very important to prevent sparking.

The high tension side of ignition systems involves very high voltages, so it is always advisable to use insulated tools wherever possible, and to avoid touching any part of the high tension system with bare hands unless you have switched off the ignition.

It is even more important when the vehicle has electronic ignition, or if you are fitting it: because of the extremely high voltages, shocks from electronic ignition systems can be very painful, and dangerous to people with, for example, a heart condition. Also be aware that ignition coils can get very hot during use, so be careful not to touch a coil after the engine has been running.

This book gives information on timing a car's engine when it is running, so make sure that you have no loose items of clothing, and that hair and jewellery cannot hang into the engine bay and risk engaging with rotating parts. Always be aware of the position of your hands and arms, keeping them at a safe distance from any moving parts. Protective eye wear is advisable.

THE BASIC PETROL ENGINE IGNITION SYSTEM

Before you get involved in any work on an automotive ignition system, you need to know the basics. Standard coil ignition is the system used on automotive petrol engines from the early 1900s to the 1980s. It is made up of a battery, a distributor, a coil, a set of high tension (HT) leads and a set of spark plugs. The battery gives power via the ignition switch to the positive terminal (on a negative earth car) on the coil; the negative terminal is connected to the low tension terminal on the distributor, this is the low tension circuit. The coil boosts the voltage to many thousands of volts and sends this through the high tension circuit via the coil lead to the distributor.

As the distributor rotates it sends high voltage down the relevant plug lead at the correct moment, to the spark plug, which makes the spark to ignite the petrol: simple! Fig. 1 shows the basic system.

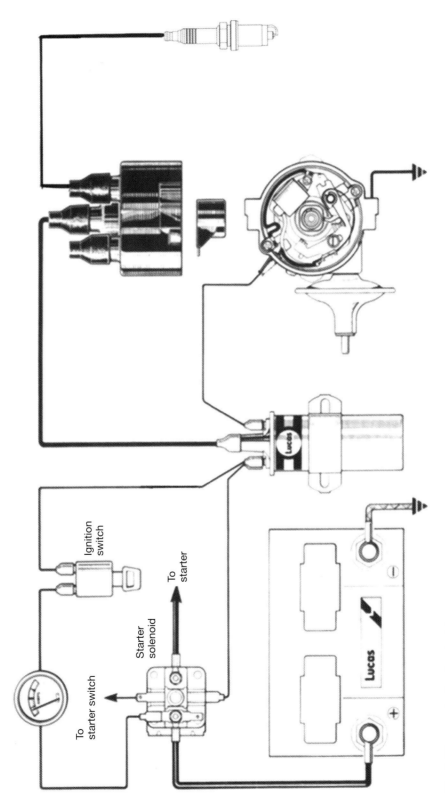

Fig. 1: The standard points ignition system. *LUCAS*

Ignition
switch

To
starter

Starter
solenoid

To
starter switch

CHAPTER ONE

HISTORY

THE EARLY DAYS

The spark plug was invented in 1860, but was not commercially available until 1902, when it was made by Robert Bosch. However, it wasn't until fifty years later that the first basic distributor made its appearance. Prior to the distributor, the ignition system was magneto-based.

MAGNETO-BASED SYSTEMS

The first magneto appeared in a car in 1899, in the Daimler Phoenix (Phonix) developed by Robert Bosch and Frederick Richard Simms; the magneto system was used in the majority of cars until about 1918, and would be used for several further years in competition cars.

A magneto relies on electro-magnetic induction, a principle that was discovered in 1831 by Michael Faraday. This basically says that if a magnet is moved within a coil of wire it will produce a spark between the ends of the wire. The scale of magneto-system manufacture can be demonstrated by the fact that by 1906 Bosch had produced 100,000 magneto systems. Magnetos generate their own electricity, therefore they are a lot lighter than having a battery, dynamo and a distributor. But with batteries becoming smaller and higher powered, manufacturers were turning to the new technology, the distributor. It is often said that the distributor system can produce a better spark at very low revs, whereas the magneto system is better suited for higher revving and does not give the same reliability at low revs.

Another drawback with the magneto system was that it had fixed timing, whereas on a distributor system the timing can be changed throughout the rev range by means of automatic or manual advance, making the engine much more efficient. Also, with the demand for more electrical equipment to be fitted to the car, and higher powered lights, it was much more sensible to have a dynamo to generate electricity and a battery to store it.

Fig. 2 shows an M.L. magneto with a Simms coupling. The Simms coupling provided a connection between the magneto and the engine. It consisted of two metal-toothed plates with a central, rubber-like section: this was slightly flexible in order to take up any shock. Simms also made very reliable magnetos. Other British companies making good magnetos at this time were Lucas, B.T.H. and M.L. However, the Swiss, Scintilla magnetos were a very highly respected unit, popular with top quality road and racing cars.

EARLY IGNITION SYSTEMS

In 1911 Cadillac were the first production company to use distributor and coil ignition. This had been developed by the Dayton Engineering Laboratories Company, now known as Delco. More commonly known as 'coil ignition' this system was originally known as the 'Kettering System' after Charles Franklin Kettering, who later became the vice president of General Motors. Kettering was the man responsible for developing the dynamo and the starter motor, giving rise to the basic components of the modern ignition system as we know them. These components would be the basis of the automotive ignition system for the next sixty years.

The distributor ignition system on vehicles up to the late 1920s was very basic, but it is important to understand the origins of the ignition system to understand later developments in the field. From the late 1920s the majority of British classic cars used Lucas ignition, while Delco were still prominent in the USA and on certain cars in the UK. In Europe, Magneti Marelli and Bosch were two of the main manufacturers.

The DJ4 and DJ6

Although Lucas made many types of distributor in the mid-1920s to the early 1930s, the first models to be

Fig. 2: An M.L. magneto with a Simms coupling.

'popular' were the DJ4 and DJ6: this was essentially the same distributor but in 4- and 6-cylinder variations. There was no internal advance mechanism: it could be fitted into a mounting bracket, allowing the advance of the distributor to be manually operated by the driver, usually by means of an advance and retard lever on the steering wheel. It is very important for the ignition to be able to advance. Advancing the ignition makes the spark happen earlier, and as the speed of the engine increases, the earlier the spark needs to be. This is because the mixture of air and fuel in the combustion chamber needs an amount of time to burn, and so the faster the engine is going, the earlier the spark needs to be. We will look at distributor advance later in the book.

The contact set gap was adjustable by the bolt-style contact, as shown in Fig. 3. On these the one contact point was screwed either in or out to obtain the correct gap. Caps, rotors and contact set are still available for this kind of system.

There is not much to rebuilding such a system: the only thing you can do is re-bush them and replace the contact set, rotor, condenser and cap. Over many years of use the cams can get pitted and worn, which affects the dwell angle and causes rapid wear to the heels of the contact breakers. The heel of the contact breaker is the part that touches the rotating cam. Originally this heel was made out of fibre, but more recently manufacturers have turned to plastic; however, it is always best to use a fibre one if possible. It is advisable to check the wear on the cam before spending money on the other items, because this cannot be economically rectified.

Fig. 3: A Lucas DJ4: it is evident that these distributors were still very basic.

Fig. 4: The contact set on the left is the early 'bolt' type as fitted to the Lucas DJ4; on the right is the later, more conventional style as used on the Lucas DK4.

The DJ4 and DJ6 were soon to be subject to a radical change, one that would be used right up to the end of distributor production: automatic advance. Still called the DJ, this was a far superior unit. A new, removable Bakelite base plate was fitted, weights and springs were included, and distributors could now have individual advance curves (see page 70 for more details) tailored to the engines they were being fitted to.

Fig. 5: The internals of a Lucas 25D4.

At this point in time some distributors had vacuum units fitted to the mounting bracket of the distributor as well; these were connected via a tube to the inlet manifold or carburettor. Soon these distributors were to be replaced with the DK4 and DK6, visually very similar but with a more conventional contact set.

Fig. 5 shows the internals of the distributor. There are two weights located by pins on the bottom of the cam plate, and two springs attach this plate to the main shaft and plate – and you will notice that these springs are different to each other. The lighter, thin spring is the primary spring, and this controls the first part of the advance curve. As the shaft spins round, the weight held by this spring moves out at a controlled rate; at this point the second weight is inactive. As this spring comes to the end of its travel, the heavier spring, known as the secondary spring, takes over and the second weight starts to move. This movement allows the top shaft and cam to move in relation to the main shaft at a controlled rate, thus creating an advance curve. The maximum advance is limited by the size of the holes that the two pins sit in: these are located on the underside of the weights. On later distributors such as the Lucas 25D4, the maximum advance is limited by the length of the leading edge of the cam plate; as can be seen in Fig. 5, the cam has 16 degrees stamped into it, which means that it will give 16 degrees maximum advance.

Although there were other attempts at advance mechanisms, the weights and spring method was adopted by all the major manufacturers.

As briefly mentioned, some engines also had a vacuum unit fitted to the mounting bracket of the distributor, to give the distributor a controlled amount of advance. More in-depth details on vacuum units are given on page 16.

Coils

The other major component of the coil ignition system is the coil. This device transforms the car's battery voltage – usually 12 volts, but it can be 6 volts in earlier cars – to several thousand volts to enable the spark plugs to spark. As such high voltages are used a condenser is fitted inside the distributor to stop the points burning and to preserve their life. Some early coils had glass cases, which were filled with oil to cool them down, see Fig. 6. However, glass-cased coils soon proved totally impractical, and metal cases became the norm. There is no maintenance to be done to a coil: it either works or it doesn't, and if you have any problems with one just get an appropriate replacement.

All coils of this period are standard, low voltage coils. Although there may be many cosmetic differences, just make sure you get the correct voltage and do not get a modern electronic or ballast-resisted coil. The modern electronic coils are 'high voltage' coils and only suitable for certain electronic ignition systems. Another version of the ignition coil is the ballast-resisted coil, but these will not be 12 volts, they will be either 6 or 9 volts.

The other version of the coil is the sports coil, such as the Lucas DLB105; these are fine to use on standard systems as they are still low voltage coils, but they produce more secondary voltage. In the mid-1930s Lucas brought out the HS12 and HS6, their new sports coils available in both 12 and 6 volts. To quote from an early Lucas publication:

> Genuine Lucas Ignition Parts are designed to give the most satisfactory performance under all operating conditions. In some instances special conditions prevail, as in high performance sports cars, radio-equipped cars fitted with chokes and suppressors in the ignition circuit, and engines fitted with wide sparking-plug gaps. To meet these special requirements the new high voltage Lucas Sports Coil, attractively finished in polychromatic brown, has been designed to balance with all existing Lucas ignition systems and at the same time give a super-performance.

Fig. 6: An early glass coil: the windings inside can be clearly seen.

Fig. 7: Some of the coils that are still available.

This sports coil was used until the early 1950s, when it was replaced with the SA12, a unit that was still popular in the 1970s. This coil had a 'groove' in case the coil overheated: in certain cases coils had been known to blow themselves apart, but this groove allowed the can to expand if it ever did get to an extreme temperature.

One thing to note on coils is the HT connection: this can be either a screw or a push-in fitting. For originality, on older vehicles screw fitting would be more appropriate, and there are several old-style coils still available. Moreover with this type of coil fitting, it is advisable to keep standard copper-core ignition leads as opposed to modern carbon leads.

Although many different distributors were fitted in this period, there were no major changes on production-car distributors until after World War II.

THE POST-WAR YEARS

In the early post-war years distributors started to be made with a vacuum advance unit built in to the distributor itself, as opposed to being attached to the mounting clamp. These helped the starting and low speed running of the engine, and most production car engines adopted this system.

A vacuum unit is connected to the engine by a copper or, in later systems, plastic tube. When the engine revs it creates a greater vacuum in the pipe, which sucks on a rubber diaphragm inside the vacuum unit. This diaphragm is connected to a 'plunger', which pulls on the distributor contact breaker base plate and thus advances the ignition. Certain distributors are fitted with a vacuum retard unit, which does the opposite in that they actually retard the ignition, usually in order to conform to strict emission control laws. Over the years this diaphragm will perish and no longer hold the vacuum pressure, and therefore no longer pulls on the base plate, so no advance is achieved.

A quick test to see if your vacuum unit is working is to detach the vacuum pipe and suck on the end of the vacuum unit and just check to see if the base plate moves; but remember this test is only to see if the unit holds vacuum and to see if the diaphragm is perished or not. Just the fact that it moves does not mean that it is working correctly, and it is important to find out that it is giving the correct amount of advance at the right time. If the vacuum unit is

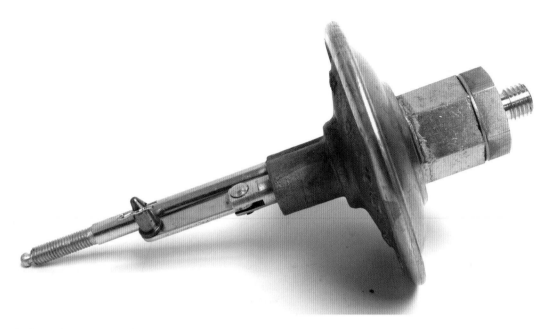

Fig. 8: One of the newly made vacuum units from the British Vacuum Unit in the USA; these are available in the UK from Retro Classic Car Parts Ltd.

not working correctly it can be sent to a specialist company such as Retro Classic Car Parts Ltd, who will either get it taken apart and the diaphragm replaced (see the photographs of this process on pages 50–52) or even better, in many cases they will be able to supply a brand new one, as shown in Fig. 8.

A new vacuum unit is the best option because of the excellent build quality of these units and the attention to detail. You can be sure they will be the correct specification for your car, which is essential, as different vacuum units will operate at different pressures and give different amounts of advance; but beware of cheap imported units, as lots of these are not made correctly and are set to the wrong specification. You may think you are getting a bargain but you are certainly not. These new units are also ideal for people who are doing a concours restoration, as they are absolutely identical to the original unit. A rebuilt unit will always stand out as being rebuilt.

Figure 9 shows that there are two sets of figures stamped into a vacuum unit. One (in this case 419681) is the part number, a six- or eight-figure number. The other set shows the operating

pressures and the total amount of advance the unit will give. The one in Fig. 9 has the numbers 4/18/12: this means that the vacuum will start operating at a pressure of 4in of mercury (4inHg), then stop at 18in of mercury (18inHg) and give a total advance of 12 degrees. The connection at the end of this vacuum is a screw thread; this is usually $\frac{5}{16}$in×24 UNF. This is then connected to the engine with a copper pipe and nut. Later vacuum units changed to a push-on fitting and used rubber pipe to connect to the engine.

In most pre-1970s distributors, when a vacuum unit is fitted there is a micrometer adjuster on one end of it, allowing for very fine adjustments to the timing – see Fig. 10. These knurled nuts basically move the vacuum unit in and out, either advancing or retarding the ignition. These nuts will wear over the years, but they have now been remade and are available again to buy.

Some distributors, such as the Aston Martin DB6 shown in Fig. 11 or the Triumph TR6 shown in Fig. 16 (UK specification shown on page 20), do not have vacuum units, they have a vacuum blank. These still have the knurled nut to adjust the fine timing,

Fig. 9: Close-up of an Aston Martin DB4 vacuum unit showing the two sets of numbers stamped into it: 419681 and 4-18-12.

Fig. 10: A Lucas DVX6A: when the knurled adjuster nut is turned, it moves the distributor base plate to advance or retard the ignition.

Fig. 11: A Lucas 25D6 from an Aston Martin DB6. Notice there is a 'blank' where the vacuum unit would usually be.

Fig. 12: A Lucas 23D4 as used on the Mini Cooper S; this style of distributor was adopted for many competition engines.

but no vacuum capsule, and cars such as the Mini Cooper S had a distributor without any vacuum or adjustment facility at all: this was the Lucas 23D4, as shown in Fig. 12.

Do not be tempted to discard your vacuum unit in a standard road-going car, as in most cases it will just lead to bad running at low RPM.

Most distributors use bushes inside the body for the main shaft to run in – see Fig. 13. These inevitably wear, and side-to-side movement starts to develop in the distributor shaft. This wear drastically degrades the performance of the distributor, which means you cannot achieve the best performance from your engine. Again, like with the vacuum units,

Fig. 13: A new bush inside a distributor body.

specialist companies can re-bush worn distributors and get them back to 'as new' performance. But in the mid-1940s another system started to become more widely used, using a roller bearing instead of the top bush, and this eliminated a lot of the wear problems – *see* Fig. 14.

Fig. 14: A Bakelite distributor base with a built-in roller bearing for the shaft to run in.

Fig. 15: The picture at the top shows the two-part points, and the one at the bottom the 'quick fit' one-part contact set.

Although this idea had been used in certain pre-war distributors, it was now to be more widely used, especially in 6- and 8-cylinder distributors, though not in many 4-cylinder versions. This use of bearings was to be used right through to the 1980s on certain distributors – for example the Jaguar V12 – but the standard bulk production units would stay with top and bottom bushes.

Apart from cosmetic changes this basic format was to stay until the 1960s, when a one-piece contact set was introduced; these were simpler to fit. They are also known as quick-fit points. Fig. 15 shows the difference between the two.

Fig. 16: The Lucas 22D6, with the rev-counter take-off drive built into the side of the body. Inside this is a gear that drives from the distributor shaft.

In certain cars, such as the Daimler V8 and the Triumphs TR5 and TR6, the distributors had an extra feature: the ability to drive a rev-counter (*see* Fig. 16).

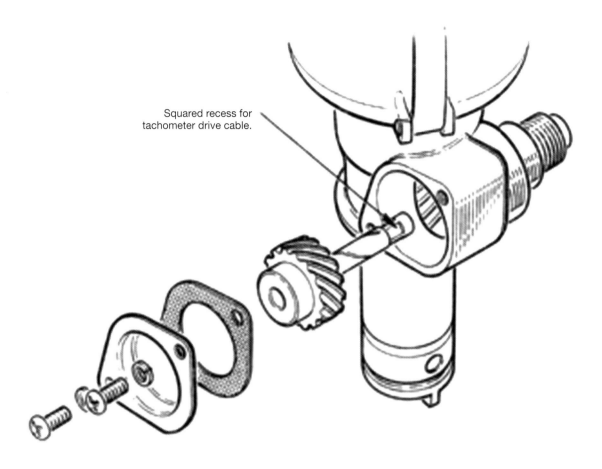

Squared recess for
tachometer drive cable.

Fig. 17: The tacho drive on the Lucas 41219 TR6 distributor. LUCAS

On the Daimler the distributor fitted into a 'tower' that housed the rev-counter drive gear, which was driven by a gear fitted to the distributor shaft. This then sent electrical pulses to the rev-counter. On the Triumph, the Lucas 22D6 distributor body had the rev-counter drive gear built in, as shown in Fig. 16, and the actual distributor shaft had a skew gear cut into it that turned the drive gear, which turned a cable that operated the rev-counter, as shown in Fig. 17. These units were made by both Lucas and Delco.

BALLAST-RESISTED SYSTEMS

Up until 1960 if you had a 12-volt car, you had a 12-volt coil; likewise with 6 volts. But there was another option now, the ballast-resisted coil system,

and one of the first production cars to use this was the Aston Martin DB4GT. In this type of system a 12-volt car would have a 6- or 9-volt coil, and a ballast resistor similar to the one shown in Fig. 18.

A ballast resistor is used to drop the voltage to the ignition after the engine has been started. So when you turn the key, 12 volts is fed to the coil, and when you release the ignition key the feed goes through the ballast resistor, reducing the voltage to match the coil. It is most important that you use the correct type of coil in this system, and if you remove the ballast resistor, make sure you change the coil for a true 12-volt coil otherwise the contact points will burn out very quickly. It is also useful to know that some ballast resistors are small and are hidden in the wiring harness.

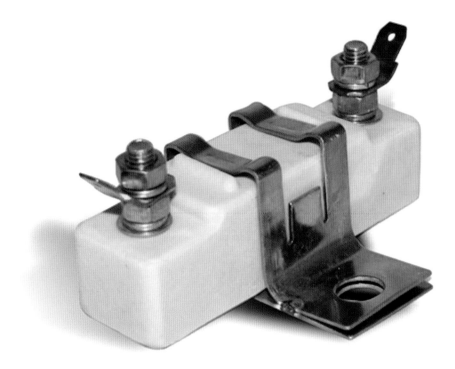

Fig. 18: A typical ballast resistor.

ELECTRONIC IGNITION

Although not available on standard production cars, certain competition cars of the early 1960s were starting to use a major breakthrough in the ignition system. In 1962 Lucas supplied transistorized electronic ignition to the BRM and Coventry Climax Formula One engines. This was seen as a massive step forward and aftermarket systems soon started to appear in the USA. Fiat was the first to actually use this technology in production cars in 1968.

There were several types of electronic ignition. The first one to mention kept the original contact breaker points but only a very low current passed through them, which greatly improved the life of the contact set. In this system there was a solid-state power pack where the high primary current was generated.

The Lucas TAC (transistor-assisted contacts) ignition system, as shown in Fig. 20, was designed to reduce the duty of the contacts, which had always imposed limitations on the performance of standard coil ignition systems. A high voltage transistor, designed especially for this purpose, is used to make and break the coil primary circuit, while the contact set carries only a small current, which operates the switching of the transistor. When this system was employed a special coil, the Lucas BA12, was used in conjunction with the 3BR ballast resistor. In this system the distributor contact breaker is connected in the transistor base circuit. When the contact set closes, a small current starts up in the base of the transistor circuit, so switching on the transistor and allowing a much larger current to flow through the ignition coil primary winding, via the collector and emitter electrodes of the transistor. When the contact set is opened, the base current is switched off and the transistor immediately becomes non-conductive; the electro-magnetic flux in the coil core collapses so that a high voltage is developed across the coil secondary winding to produce a spark at the plug in the normal manner.

The contact breaker is called upon to handle only a relatively small current, around 1–2 amps, and since

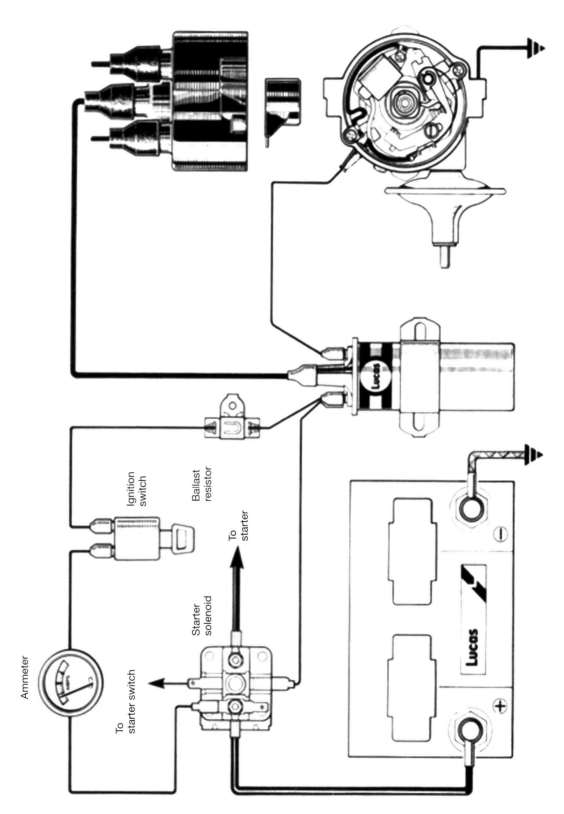

Ignition
switch

Ballast
resistor

To
starter

Starter
solenoid

Ammeter

To
starter switch

Fig. 19: The standard ballast-resisted ignition system. *LUCAS*

Fig. 20: The Lucas T.A.C. system showing the power pack, the special coil and the ballast resistor.

Fig. 21: The Aerochem Power Start unit.

the contacts' circuit is only a resistive one, instead of the highly inductive circuit with more conventional ignition, contacts' life is greatly increased. Moreover the transistor can handle a greater current and is a most efficient switch, which further permits an improved ignition performance to be obtained both at high and low speed. After the initial bedding in of the fibre heel, no further contact adjustment is needed for at least 25,000 miles, and then only to compensate for the heel wear. This system also eliminates the use of a condenser.

In the UK a company called Sparkrite was one of the main companies manufacturing an aftermarket version of this style of electronic ignition. Versions of this type of electronic ignition are still available, and we will look into them in more detail later in the book.

Another interesting product was the Aerochem Power Start from the Netherlands, see Fig. 21, a product that used a battery to boost the ignition power. This is the introduction from the Power Start fitting guide:

The Power Start Unit has been designed for installing into either the six- or twelve-volt conventional ignition system of a petrol-driven vehicle, to overcome the starting problems caused by cold, damp and many other factors which contribute to the weakening of electric power during initial ignition. The Power Start Unit ensures that during starting the ignition of the car is automatically boosted by means of a six-volt battery. This, of course, does not alter the fact that normal maintenance of the ignition system must take place regularly.

When installing the Power Start Unit, spark plugs and contact points must be in good functional condition, and the ignition wiring and distributor clean and dry. The Power Start Unit is suitable for all types of petrol-driven engines with a six- or twelve-volt battery – positive or negative earth. The unit can be installed either in the engine compartment (preferably) or in the interior of the car. An on–off switch is supplied, which may be fitted either in or under the dashboard by means of the supporting panel. The wiring used must have a core of 14/012in. The cable shoes supplied with the apparatus must be firmly crimped on to the bared ends by means of pliers and soldered if necessary.

This was an interesting idea but not one that took off. The other systems did not use contact breaker points at all.

LUCAS OPUS (OSCILLATING PICK-UP SYSTEM) IGNITION SYSTEM

The OPUS ignition was developed in the mid-1960s for the Cosworth V8 Formula One engine. There was no other ignition system available at the time that could provide the accurate and rapid high coil switching currents as required for high-revving multi-cylinder engines. This type of electronic ignition is known as 'constant dwell'. The term 'dwell' in a standard contact-breaker ignition system refers to the length of time that the points are closed, whereas in this system it is the length of time that the transistor is switched on. As the engine speed increases, the dwell remains the same.

OPUS ignition amplifiers came in a few formats; some were mounted in the distributor, including Rolls Royce, Rover and MG. The Cosworth V8, Jaguar V12 and the Aston Martin V8 used the OPUS Type AB3, where the amplifier was mounted externally from the distributor. The AB3 amplifier was a die-cast aluminium unit with a set of cooling fins on the top, as shown in Fig. 22.

The OPUS amplifier has an oscillator running at about 550kHZ to provide the excitation for the pick-up. The OPUS pick-up is a small transformer with three windings on an open-ended, E-shaped ferrite core. The moulded nylon distributor rotor carries ferrite rods, spaced one per cylinder around its circumference; as each rod passes the pick-up (0.020thou gap), a magnetic loop is created in the upper winding of the E core, producing a voltage output from the pick-up. The resulting voltage pulses are transmitted to the amplifier, which switches the coil current *off*, generating the HT spark from the ignition coil secondary winding. When no ferrite rod is opposite the pick-up, the ignition coil current will be *on*, re-energizing the coil. Remember the spark is produced when the coil is switched *off*. The collapsing magnetic field in the ignition coil creates a high voltage in the coil secondary windings providing the spark.

In 1971 the OPUS AB3 ignition amplifier entered the production car market fitted to the Jaguar V12, Aston Martin V8 and many other performance engines. All V12 E-types were originally supplied with the amplifier mounted in the V, as shown in Fig. 22. The pick-up and amplifier wiring was black with coloured bands. Some later Jaguar and Daimler V12 saloons and Jaguar XJS cars were supplied with six coloured wires, and the amplifier was usually mounted on the front chassis rail away from the engine. The cars fitted with the five-wire amplifiers with coloured wiring were a replacement OPUS and used a different ballast resistor block. The difference was that the tachometer was triggered from the

Fig. 22: The OPUS amplifier mounted in the 'V' of a Jaguar V12 engine.

coil negative via a higher value resistor. The OPUS system was renowned for suffering with heat problems, and it was believed that mounting the amplifier away from the engine would fix these problems.

Suitable 'cost-effective', high temperature and stable components were not available at the time, and when coupled with the differing pick-up characteristics made the OPUS difficult to calibrate to ensure reliability for the long term.

The OPUS pick-up/amplifier is a resonant circuit: the pick-up and amplifier must be in tune with each other for it to work. It is like tuning your radio for the correct station: if it is not correctly tuned the output will be distorted. The amplifier/oscillator frequency is critical: a change of 10 per cent in the wrong direction and the ignition will fail. If you change the pick-up wiring length, in most instances it will upset the circuit balance.

OPUS problems have been well documented over the years, some justified and some from individuals who didn't realize that the days when the local blacksmith could fix your car without reading the service manual were fast disappearing. Apart from age and the quality of the components used, some of the OPUS problems were due to poor maintenance including incorrect pick-up gap, failure to keep connectors clean, fuel pump, carburettor tuning and 'experts' changing the wiring.

Electronic components have a lifetime. The original OPUS amplifier used 85°C rated components in the engine bay: your amplifier could be operating at more than 95°C and therefore above the component's designed temperature range, and this was a recipe for disaster! Fortunately electronic components have vastly improved over the last forty years. Keeping the ignition system, wiring and ballast block as original as possible is important, so it can then be maintained as per the manufacturer's repair manual if possible. A V12 engine does require careful and precise maintenance practices, and the manufacturer's maintenance manual will always be the most reliable and honest source of information. If your car is maintained as per manual, this ensures that it can be repaired by a competent technician in the future.

Fig. 23: On the left, an original OPUS timing rotor; on the right is a nylon replacement.

If you do decide to change how the ignition operates, keep all the documentation in a folder and keep all the original parts. The next owner or repairer may wish to return the ignition to the original at some time.

The most common fault with the OPUS ignition is an incorrect pick-up gap: it must be 0.020in, and if this does not work there are other component problems. There are two types of pick-up: the original with black wires, and the later OPUS with coloured wires; their output characteristics are almost the same, but they have a different plug gender. The OPUS pick-up has three very small coils wound with 0.0055in wire; these windings are not protected from the environment in the distributor, and some have changed their impedance more than others over the years. This does cause ignition trigger problems, in that many pick-ups have become very hot, and their values have changed; we also see pick-ups with broken E cores, probably due to incorrect pick-up to rotor gap. It must be 0.020in for the original timing rotor.

Some OPUS amplifiers are still working today, almost forty years since manufacture. How many electronic devices do you have that still work after forty years?

There is a nylon replacement rotor available, as shown in Fig. 23: the ferrite rods are about 0.008in further in from the edge than the original rotors, while the nylon timing rotors reduce the pick-up gap to suit.

There are two different distributor rotor arms used on OPUS systems: a tapered rotor for the carburettor engines and a rotor that has a magnet moulded in the square end for the fuel injection system, as shown in Fig. 24.

Fig. 24: On the left, a rotor from a carburettor engine; on the right, from a fuel injection engine.

Fig. 25: A 9BR ballast resistor.

There are four different ballast resistor blocks, and they all look the same but differ internally. Two are for the original six-wire amplifiers: Lucas 9BR Y4722A and 9BR Y47229A, see Fig 25. One is for the later replacement five-wire amplifier: Lucas 9BR 47246A; and the last is for a replacement ignition system where the ballast block has LUCAS 9BR stamped on to it, but has no other numbers: this ballast block is for use with the replacement amplifier and special coil only.

The rev-counter trigger connection for a five-wire system is taken via a resistor from the coil negative. If you do not have the correct ballast block do not connect the coil negative directly to the early ballast resistors Type 9BR Y4722A and 9BR Y47229A, as this applies 12 volts to the coil negative via the 8ohm resistor and then a very weak spark is produced and the engine will not start.

The ballast resistor block part numbers' internal resistance values and connection information is documented on www.reopusignition.com.

Suitable coils are still available. The original coil has a 0.8ohm primary resistance, but a high-performance coil suitable for use with an external ballast resistor with a primary resistance less than 1.3ohm and a 100:1 secondary to primary turns ratio will work satisfactorily.

CONSTANT ENERGY IGNITION

In the constant energy system the dwell angle increases with engine speed. These ignition systems use very low resistance coils, such as the Lucas DLB198. These have a primary resistance of about 1ohm. Fig. 26 is a drawing of a Lucas 35DLM8: notice that the amplifier is screwed directly to the side of the body.

The amplifier in these systems can work out when the primary circuit needs to be switched on. This means that the dwell angle and the period are automatically adjusted to suit the needs of the engine, which in turn means that the output energy to the spark plug remains constant through the whole rev range. This system is much better than the constant dwell system and quickly replaced it in the production car market due to its better performance and its ability to meet modern emission laws.

OPTICAL ELECTRONIC IGNITION

The other main system available is an optical system, such as Lumenition, used in aftermarket fitments. This system works by creating a beam of light inside the distributor, which is broken by a fan-like blade, called a chopper, fitted over the distributor cam. As the distributor rotates, the chopper blade breaks the beam of light, and the optical switch and external power module fire the coil and generate a very powerful spark: there is one blade for each of the engine's cylinders. See Fig. 27.

We will look further into this electronic ignition system in the modifications section of the book.

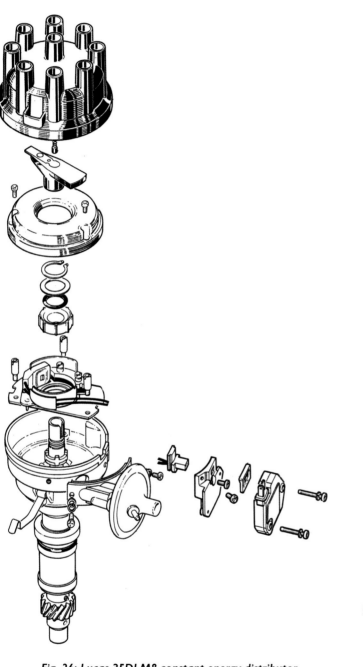

Fig. 26: Lucas 35DLM8 constant energy distributor.

LUCAS

Fig. 27: A Lumenition optical switch and chopper blade fitted inside a Motorcraft distributor.

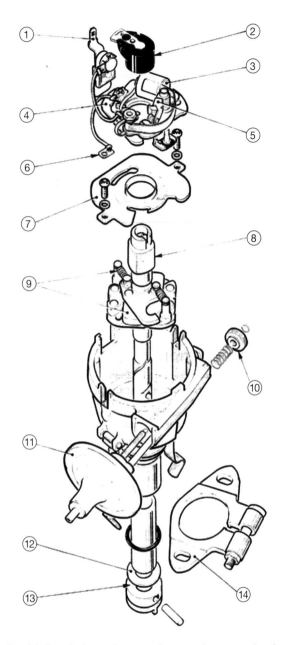

1 LT terminal
2 Rotor arm
3 Capacitor
4 Contact breaker moving plate
5 Contact set
6 Contact breaker earth terminal
7 Contract breaker base plate
8 Cam
9 Automatic advance springs and weights
10 Micrometer adjustment nut
11 Vacuum unit
12 Thrust washer
13 Drive dog and pin
14 Securing plate

Fig. 28: Break-down diagram showing the internals of a Lucas 25D4 distributor. LUCAS

DISTRIBUTOR COMPONENTS

CONTACT SET

The contact set, also known as the points, acts as a switch for the ignition coil. When the contact set closes, a small electrical current flows through them, and this then triggers the coil to release high voltage current to the relative spark plug. As the shaft in the distributor rotates, the lobes on the cam open the contact set at precisely the right time.

It is essential to get the correct gap between the points for an engine to run correctly. The size of this gap can usually be found in the owner's manual.

To measure the gap in the contact set, you will need a set of feeler gauges (*see* Fig. 29). First, make sure the heel of the contact set is on the high point of one of the cam lobes. If it isn't, you will have to slightly turn the engine in order to turn the distributor cam. This can be done by operating the starter, but this is very inaccurate and can take several attempts to get the cam in the right position. The other method, and by far the best, is to turn the engine by hand – nice and easy for those of you with starting handles! This can be done by turning the crankshaft pulley with a spanner on the central pulley bolt. Make sure the car is in neutral and turn clockwise (to avoid loosening the bolt) until the cam is in the correct position and the contact set is fully open.

Slightly loosen the adjustment screw holding the contact set to the base plate. Insert your feeler gauge, set to the correct setting, and with a screwdriver adjust the contacts so that they just touch the blade of the feeler gauge. Tighten the adjustment screw and re-check: if it is not right, repeat the process until the correct gap is achieved.

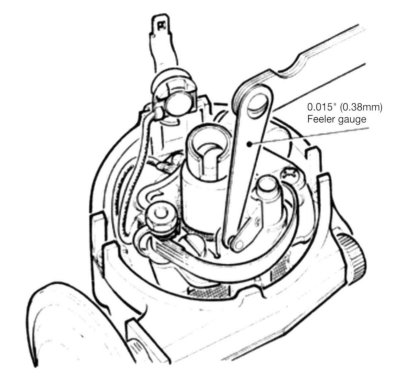

0.015" (0.38mm)
Feeler gauge

*Fig. 29: The points gap being
measured with a feeler gauge.*

LUCAS

CONDENSER

The condenser is usually located inside the distributor, screwed down to the base plate, but on certain distributors it is mounted on the outside of the distributor body (*see* Fig. 31).

The purpose of the condenser is to cause a more rapid collapse of the magnetic field inside the coil, which then boosts the secondary voltage induced. As the condenser is fitted in parallel with the contact set, when the contact set opens, the primary voltage, instead of trying to jump the contact gap, goes through the condenser. The current going through the condenser builds up an electrostatic charge. It then discharges back through the coil and starts to be recharged again. The induced energy in the primary circuit is then dissipated causing very little damage to the contacts. If the condenser were not in the circuit the contact points would burn rapidly.

*Fig. 30: A Lucas DCB101
condenser, a very popular unit.*

Fig. 31: An early Ford distributor; the condenser is mounted on the outside of the unit, a mounting style also used by Delco.

Condensers are usually an easy part to replace: on most distributors you simply unscrew them from the base plate and fit another. In certain cases, however, for example the Lucas DKY4A, they are actually soldered to the base plate. Originally, in these cases, when you needed to replace the condenser you replaced the whole unit, condenser and base plate. Never be tempted to unsolder the condenser and solder in a new one, as this will just cause damage to the internals of the condenser. The best option here is to cut off the condenser, drill and tap the base plate, and then fit a standard screw-on style condenser.

ROTOR ARM

The rotor arm has a metal blade, which contacts the central high voltage cable from the coil via a carbon and spring inside the distributor cap. As the distributor rotates, the blade of the rotor arm passes close to (but does not touch) the terminals inside the distributor cap, which are connected via

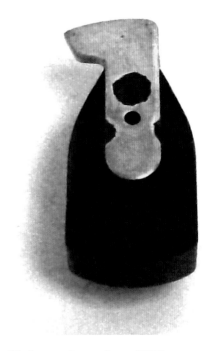

Fig. 32: A rotor from a Lucas 25D6 amongst other 6-cylinder distributors.

the HT leads to the spark plugs. As the rotor spins within the distributor, electrical current is able to jump the small gaps created between the rotor arm and the contacts due to the high voltage created by the ignition coil.

COIL

An ignition coil is basically a type of transformer. It has no moving parts and consists of two sets of windings. The primary windings are made of quite a heavy wire and there are only about 300 turns of them, whereas the secondary windings are made of about 20,000 turns of fine wire, each layer being insulated from the next. It is needed to boost the car's low tension voltage, usually 12 volts, to at least 10,000 volts, and on an engine that is revving at 4,500rpm the coil has to do this 150 times per second on a 4-cylinder engine!

This is done by a process called magnetic induction, where a coil of wire is wound round an iron core and a current is passed through it: this causes a magnetic field to be produced, making the iron core into a magnet. When the current is switched off, the magnetic field collapses and induces a reverse current in the coil. When a second coil is wound on top of the first coil, as the field collapses a current will be induced into it. If the number of turns in the second coil is greater than in the first coil, then the voltage in the second coil will be greater than the supply voltage. This is basically how the step up in voltage is produced.

Fig. 33: A typical coil.

DISTRIBUTOR CAP

A distributor cap is the cover of the distributor; it can be made of Bakelite or certain modern plastics. Either brass or aluminium posts are moulded into the cap, one for each of the car's cylinders and a central one that connects internally to a carbon brush via a spring. When fitted, this carbon brush makes contact with the rotor arm. The HT leads can enter the cap from either the top or the side (see Fig. 34).

Fig. 34: Two distributor caps: the one on the left takes in the HT leads vertically; the one on the right is a side entry style.

CHAPTER TWO

MAINTENANCE AND REBUILDING

STANDARD MAINTENANCE

An ignition system must be regularly maintained to optimize performance, reliability and economy from the engine.

CONTACT SET

The first item to check is the contact set: make sure the contacts are in good condition and that the contact set gap is correct, and that the contact points are clean and free from oil or grease. When the heel of the contact set is on one of the lobes of the cam, thus making them fully open, set the points gap by inserting a feeler gauge with the engine's recommended setting; tighten the screw holding the contact set, pull out the feeler gauge and then double check – see Fig. 35.

As the engine turns, the contact set opens and closes: the amount of time they are closed is known as the 'dwell angle', and this is measured in degrees. The length of time the contact set is closed is needed for the primary windings in the coil to reach their desired value. The dwell angle is inversely proportional to the contact set gap, so by increasing the contact set gap you decrease the dwell. The dwell can be checked with a dwell meter, of which there are various types available; a good hand-held automotive multimeter such as the Gunson G4187 is ideal (see Fig. 36).

Fig. 35: A contact set gap being checked using a feeler gauge.

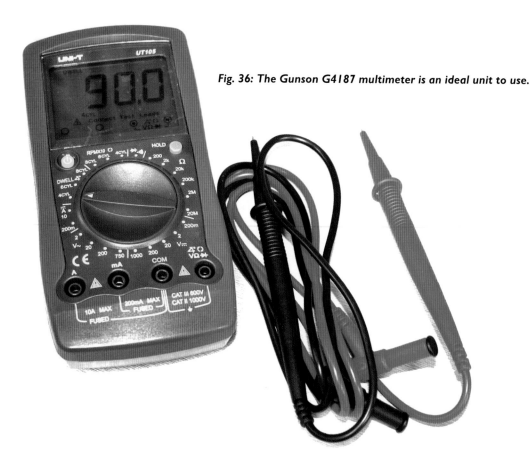

Fig. 36: The Gunson G4187 multimeter is an ideal unit to use.

Otherwise some good strobe lights such as the Gunson Supastrobe G4123 have a built-in facility to measure the dwell angle. For example, a Lucas 4-cylinder 25D4 distributor has a dwell angle of 60 degrees with an official tolerance of 3 degrees, whereas a Lucas 6-cylinder 25D6 will have a dwell angle of 35 degrees and the same tolerance of 3 degrees.

On a twin-point distributor, as shown in Fig. 37, it will be necessary to adjust the dwell on each set individually. Make sure they are both the same.

The photographs in Fig. 38 show the difference between a good and bad contact set: the bad set is burned and pitted and deposits have built up on the surface of the contact, whereas the other is nice and clean. You can scrape off the deposits and clean the contacts with either a points file or emery paper. Draper make a great little points file, as shown in Fig. 39; attached to it are also two feeler gauges, one

for 0.025in and the other for 0.015in. When filing the contacts it is important to make sure they are level and flat, and that they close nicely together. If they are too badly pitted they should be replaced, if possible.

ROTOR ARMS

Most people check and clean their points, but what about the other parts? Rotor arms and caps are often overlooked but are just as important to check.

The picture in Fig. 40 of the two rotor arms again shows one good one and one that needs replacing. It is advisable to replace rotors and caps rather than trying to clean them. Scraping the deposits away and filing rotors and caps increases the gap that the spark has to jump, so if they are in bad condition, replace them. When replacing rotor arms try to obtain one where the blade is bonded to the body, not riveted – see Fig. 41 – as these are much more reliable.

Fig. 37: A twin-point distributor from a Daimler V8.

Fig. 38: The difference between a new and an old set of points.

DISTRIBUTOR

After about 6,000 miles a distributor is in need of a clean and some general lubrication.

The inside of the cap can be cleaned with a soft dry cloth; pay attention to the areas between the metal electrodes. These electrodes need to be checked for erosion; also check that the carbon brush in the centre of the cap is not broken or cracked.

The cam needs lubrication, and it is recommended to use a light grease. Make sure that the

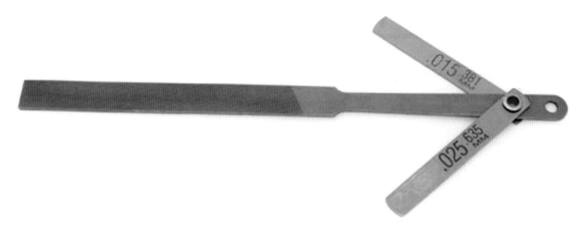

Fig. 39: The Draper points file comes with two feeler gauges, one at 0.015in and one at 0.025in.

Fig. 40: The difference between the new and the old rotor arm is clear to see.

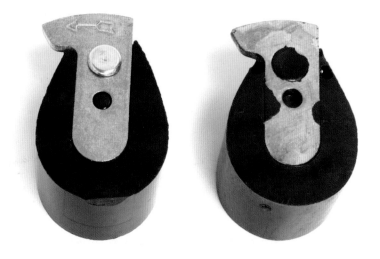

Fig. 41: Two rotor arms: on the left a rivet holds the blade on; on the right it is bonded directly to the body: these are much better.

Fig. 42: The felt plug situated over the cam mounting screw.

base plate can move freely, and in the case of a two-part base plate, apply a couple of drops of an engine oil such as SAE30. This same oil can be used to lubricate the fitting of the cam to the shaft. Look in the top of the shaft: there should be a screw visible, though it may well be covered by a small piece of felt – see Fig. 42.

Put a couple of drops of SAE30 on to this screw: this will let the cam turn freely on the shaft.

Spark plugs also suffer from deposits building up and affecting their performance and should be cleaned regularly. This is usually done with a wire brush, but you can achieve a much better result by using a Gunson spark-plug cleaner operated by a compressor – see Fig. 43.

This cleaner has a two-way valve so that you can use abrasive cleaning and air cleaning. It can clean not only the inner electrode but also the spark-plug outer area and the inner insulator as well, to give the best results – ideal if your plugs are rare and hard to replace.

Make sure that you move the spark plug from side to side so that all areas are cleaned by the grit (see Figs 44, 45, 46).

Remember you must be sure to reset the gap on the spark plug electrode to the recommended setting using a feeler gauge, see Fig. 47. If the gap is too large, a gentle tap of the electrode on a hard surface will slightly close it – though remember, not too hard! If the gap is too small then carefully open it with a small screwdriver.

The gap adjustment can be fairly critical, and if it is badly adjusted the engine may run badly, or not at all. A narrow gap may give too small and weak a spark to effectively ignite the fuel-air mixture, while a gap that is too wide might prevent a spark from firing at all. Again, if in doubt just replace them, making sure you get the correct ones for your engine.

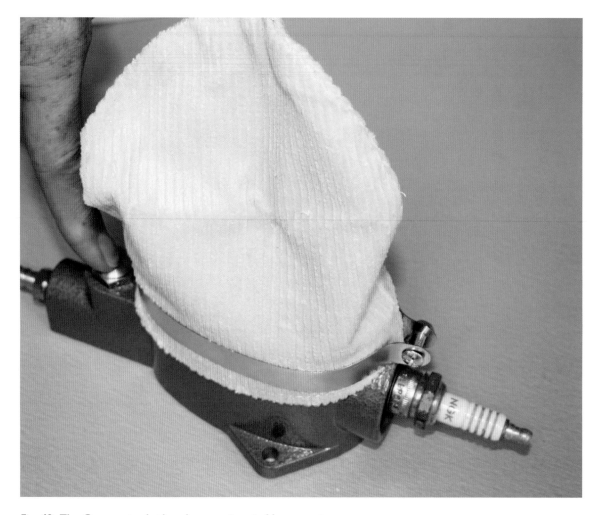

Fig. 43: The Gunson spark-plug cleaner, operated by a compressor.

Make sure that all the ignition leads are in good condition and not damaged in any way. Any leads that are damaged must be replaced. The pictures in Fig. 48 show a washer and nut being fitted to copper-core HT lead for use with a screw-fitting distributor cap.

If you have a 'push-in' fitting cap then you will need to use a special crimping tool to get the best results (*see* Fig. 49); this gives a very strong connection. (For more details on ignition leads, *see* pages 60–62.)

OTHER THINGS TO CHECK

Other things to check when maintaining the ignition system are the LT leads, as these are very delicate and are prone to breaking. Apart from the main LT connection into the distributor, some distributors have the same type of wire connecting the base plates: as this is constantly moving, it often frays and breaks. Figure 50 shows a two-part base plate with a very fine lead connecting the two: if this has to be replaced make sure that the wire used is not too stiff, as this may affect the movement of the top plate, which must be able to move freely.

The next thing to check is really the most important. With the cap and rotor off, hold the cam firmly

Figs 44, 45, 46: A spark plug inside the Gunson cleaner: moving the spark plug from left to right ensures that it is cleaned properly.

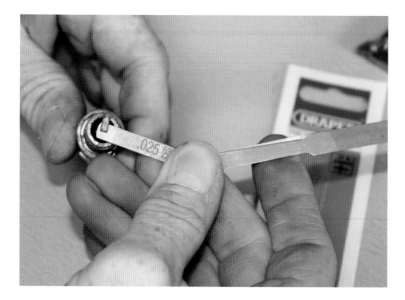

Fig. 47: Checking the spark-plug gap with a set of feeler gauges.

Fig. 48: A copper washer and distributor-cap nut fitted to some copper-core HT lead.

Fig. 49: The special HT terminal crimping tool.

Fig. 50: A Lucas 25D4 distributor base plate.

and see if there is any side-to-side movement: if this is excessive it is a sign of wear in the bushes, and the only option is to rebuild the distributor or replace it.

REBUILDING A DISTRIBUTOR

The best advice for distributor rebuilding is 'leave it to the professionals', because if a distributor is incorrectly rebuilt you can cause more harm than good. Apart from getting correct tolerances, setting the

correct advance curve and vacuum settings is absolutely crucial to the optimum running of the engine. Retro Classic Car Parts Ltd offer a rebuilding service for all points-type distributors, and they make sure that all units are set to the exact manufacturer's specifications, and not just re-bushed and cleaned!

The following photographs show the complete rebuilding of a forty-year-old Lucas 25D4 unit.

Figure 51 shows a typical forty-year-old distributor. This is in need of a total rebuild. The first thing

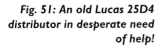

Fig. 51: An old Lucas 25D4 distributor in desperate need of help!

Fig. 52: The Lucas 25D4 completely stripped.

to do is to strip the unit completely (*see* Fig. 52), making sure not to lose any of the small screws and so on, as they can be very hard to replace. The rotor arm, condenser and contact set can go straight in the bin if new ones are available. On distributors such as the one shown, take special care when removing the vacuum unit as there is a small spring clip behind the knurled nut; this puts a slight pressure on the nut to stop it from just freely turning. However, don't worry too much if you do lose this clip as these are now remanufactured along with the knurled nut.

In this type of distributor there are two bushes in the body, one at the top of the shaft housing as shown in Fig. 53, and one at the bottom.

These are carefully pressed out and discarded. The body is then cleaned and bead blasted to give a nice finish, as shown in Fig. 54. The weights (steel ones only), base plate, drive dog, cap clips and cam are also cleaned and blasted, and plated where required. Lead weights are just cleaned and checked for wear on the mounting holes. Two new bushes are pressed in and honed to give the correct fit for the shaft.

Always check that the shaft is perfectly straight before refitting, *see* Fig. 55. If the shaft is found to be not straight, the best thing to do is replace it – though note that the shafts in clockwise-rotating distributors are different to those in anti-clockwise rotating ones, and must be replaced like for like.

Fig. 53: The old 25D4 distributor body showing the bush in the centre.

Fig. 54: The distributor body has now been bead blasted and a new central bush fitted.

Fig. 55: The distributor shaft is run up in a lathe to check that it is straight.

The shaft is then assembled. First place the weights into position on the action plate, see Fig. 56.

The cam is then fitted on to the shaft, making sure that the locating pins fit correctly into the weights.

Carefully attach the springs between the posts on the action plate and the posts on the base of the cam, as shown in Fig. 57.

On the type of distributor we are rebuilding here, the cam has a number stamped on the base plate, see Fig. 58. This indicates the total amount of advance that this specific cam will give: here it is 15 degrees. Basically the length of this protruding part of the base determines this, and the longer it is, the less advance it will be able to give because it will not be able to rotate as far before it hits the post. If the arm is shorter, however, it will be able to turn further, thus giving more advance. Don't always take it for granted that the figure stamped on the base is correct, as it may have been modified at some time in its life. Filing the plate will make it shorter, to give more maximum advance, whereas welding extra on to the end of the plate will make it longer, resulting in less maximum advance.

Replace the special screw that holds the cam to the shaft.

When the shaft is fitted back in the body, make sure not to forget the plastic cupped washer that sits under the action plate, as shown in Fig. 59.

Figure 60 shows an A-series drive dog being fitted: this is done with a steel pin that goes through the holes in the drive dog and through the hole in the shaft. If the old one has excessive wear, then replace it with a new one. Some distributors use a skew gear or a drive shaft, and these must also be checked for wear. The drive dog must be fitted correctly, making sure not to fit it the wrong way round. If you look at the driving tongues on the dog you will see that they are not central, they are offset. Think of it as a large 'D' and a small 'D'.

Fig. 56: The weights are now placed in position on the distributor shaft.

Fig. 57: Re-fit the cam and attach the advance springs.

Fig. 58: A distributor cam: the maximum advance figure is stamped on the base.

Fig. 59: The shaft is now fitted back into the distributor body – don't forget the washer!

Fig. 60: 'Big D – little D'. Notice how the drive dog is fitted, with the large 'D' to the left, and the small 'D' to the right.

Fig. 61: The relationship between the rotor-blade position and the drive dog.

Hold the distributor in your hand so that you can see the rotor mounting slot in the cam and also the drive dog. With the slot on the cam facing you, the big 'D' should be on the left, as shown in Fig. 61.

Between the drive dog and the distributor body there is a washer. The original new washers had three dimples on one side and three corresponding pips on the other, and the washer should be fitted with the pips facing away from the body and towards the drive dog. The dog is then fitted and pinned to the shaft so that it is a tight fit. Then tap the end of the shaft with a soft-faced hammer: this flattens the pips and gives the correct amount of end float, enabling the shaft to turn freely. If a new washer is not available then the correct gap between the drive dog and washer is 0.002in (0.05mm).

Fit the distributor base plate back on with the two correct mounting screws, remembering to connect the base-plate lead with one of the screws: see Fig. 62.

The next thing to fit is the vacuum unit. Fit a new one if possible, but if not, old ones can be rebuilt. This involves opening the capsule, as shown in Fig. 63.

When the unit is split open, remove the diaphragm, spring and plunger. Figure 64 shows the individual parts once the unit is split.

The two halves of the capsule can then be blasted and plated and the diaphragm replaced: see Fig. 65.

Fig. 62: The distributor base plate is now fitted with the two locating screws.

Fig. 63: An old vacuum unit positioned in a lathe. This will then be turned and cut to split the vacuum in half.

Fig. 64: The old vacuum unit is now split into separate parts.

Fig. 65: The two halves of the vacuum unit have now been replated, and a new diaphragm is to be fitted.

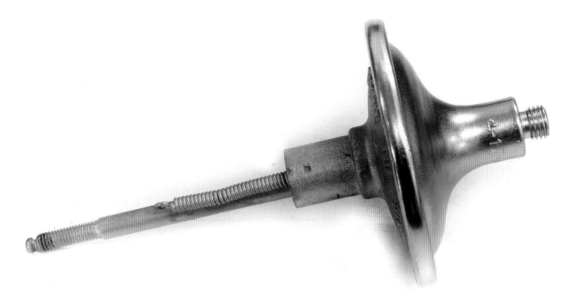

Fig. 66: The reconditioned vacuum unit is now ready to fit.

This is then reassembled and a sealing ring fitted to hold it together and seal the unit.

The end result will be a perfectly usable vacuum unit, as shown in Fig. 66.

Fit the vacuum unit back into the body, as shown in Fig. 67, locating the spring on the vacuum over the peg on the distributor base plate. Fit the small spring clip to the distributor body, taking care not to lose it.

Slot the spring over the threaded end of the vacuum unit and replace the knurled nut (see Fig. 68). Finally fit the new contacts, condenser, low tension lead and rotor. Set the gap in the contacts to the recommended setting; this will be found in the owner's handbook or a good car manual.

Now fit a new distributor cap.

The distributor is now fully assembled but needs testing, as shown in Fig. 70, and the advance curve needs checking and if not correct, re-setting. As mentioned, each distributor has its own advance curve and it is essential that this is correct to match your engine.

This can only be done with specialized equipment, as shown in Fig. 70. Originally each distributor had its own pair of springs, which were available to buy as spare parts. Nowadays, when a distributor is rebuilt, springs are 'tweaked' to obtain the correct advance curve. Many people, when rebuilding a distributor, just put the old springs back in and think that all will be perfect, but this is not the case, as old springs stretch and weaken with age. Also, if they have been taken off several times they will probably be damaged, and this then creates an incorrect advance curve. A specialist rebuilder, even if using the old springs, will alter them making sure they perform correctly.

See page 71 for an advance curve sample and how to test it.

Once this is done the distributor is ready to fit back into your car.

Fig. 67: Fit the vacuum unit back into the distributor body. Notice the small spring clip fitted to the body, just to the right of the spring.

Fig. 68: Secure the vacuum with the knurled nut.

Fig. 69: Final assembly with new cap fitted.

Fig. 70: Now the distributor can be tested and the advance curve checked. If the curve is not correct, now is the time to set it.

TWIN-POINT DISTRIBUTORS

Certain distributors from as far back as the late 1920s had two sets of contact points. There are basically two types. If we take 6 cylinders as an example, some early distributors had a three-lobe cam and two sets of contacts, while others would have a six-lobe cam with two sets of contacts; Delco used both types. On a three-lobe cam distributor there is one set of contacts opening for each spark.

When a 6-cylinder distributor has a six-lobe cam or an 8-cylinder has an eight-lobe cam, as shown in Fig. 37, it gets a bit more complicated.

When a 6- or 8-cylinder engine is running at high revs, one set of contacts will suffer from bounce, so two sets are fitted on opposing sides of the cam; these are electrically connected and are fitted slightly out of phase with each other. The first set of points (the primary set) opens, and before it closes the second set (secondary set) opens. This means that the primary set of points opens the circuit and the secondary set closes it: thus two sets of points share the work for one 'spark'. This means that they wear less and last longer.

This system has been used successfully with 6- and 8-cylinder engines in competition, but not so much with 4 cylinders. We will look more at these later in the book when we discuss modifications.

CHAPTER THREE

SPARK PLUGS AND IGNITION LEADS

SPARK PLUGS

Another major part of the ignition system is the spark plug.

A spark plug is an electrical device that fits into the cylinder head of some internal combustion engines and ignites compressed aerosol gasoline by means of an electric spark. Spark plugs have an insulated centre electrode, which is connected by a heavily insulated wire to an ignition coil or magneto circuit on the outside, forming, with a grounded terminal on the base of the plug, a spark gap inside the cylinder.

Internal combustion engines can be divided into spark-ignition engines, which require spark plugs to begin combustion, and compression-ignition engines (diesel engines), which compress the air and then inject diesel fuel into the heated compressed air mixture where it auto-ignites. Compression-ignition engines may use glow plugs to improve cold-start characteristics.

The spark plug has two primary functions:

- To ignite the air/fuel mixture. Electrical energy is transmitted through the spark plug, jumping the gap in the plug's firing end if the voltage supplied to the plug is high enough. This electrical spark ignites the gasoline/air mixture in the combustion chamber
- To remove heat from the combustion chamber. Spark plugs cannot create heat, they can only remove heat. The temperature of the end of the plug's firing end must be kept low enough to prevent pre-ignition, but high enough to prevent fouling. The spark plug works as a heat exchanger by pulling unwanted thermal energy from the combustion chamber and transferring heat to the engine's cooling system. The heat range of a spark plug is defined according to its ability to dissipate heat from the tip

OPERATION

The plug is connected to the high voltage generated by an ignition coil or magneto. As the electrons flow from the coil, a voltage difference develops between the centre electrode and side electrode. No current can flow because the fuel and air in the gap is an insulator, but as the voltage rises further, it begins to change the structure of the gases between the electrodes. Once the voltage exceeds the dielectric strength of the gases in the combustion chamber, the gases become ionized. The ionized gas becomes a conductor and allows electrons to flow across the gap. Spark plugs usually require voltage in excess of 20,000 volts to 'fire' properly.

As the current of electrons surges across the gap, it raises the temperature of the spark channel to 60,000K. The intense heat in the spark channel causes the ionized gas to expand very quickly, like a small explosion. This is the 'click' heard when observing a spark, similar to lightning and thunder.

CHOOSING SPARK PLUGS

When choosing spark plugs there are many options from many different manufacturers, and making the right choice is critical for an engine to run at its best. Most British classic cars would have had Champion or Lodge spark plugs as original equipment, and the correct one would be identified in the owner's handbook. You will find some original fitting recommendations in the Appendix.

Figure 71 shows an early spark plug. This type of plug would come apart for cleaning, and was a system used until the mid-1950s. After this, spark plugs were in one piece and it was no longer possible to take them apart. Spark plugs have model numbers printed on the side for identification.

All the letters and numbers in the individual spark-plug model number have a meaning. In the Appendix you will find the Champion, Lodge and

Fig. 71: An early Lodge spark plug; these came apart for cleaning and were supplied in a nice tin box.

NGK alphanumeric identifications. It is important to understand more about spark plugs at this stage, as a correct knowledge of the product will help you to make the right choice when replacing them, and to perhaps choose something better than you have been using.

The first thing to understand is the difference between 'hot' and 'cold' plugs. Basically a cold plug is a hard plug, and a hot plug is a soft plug. Cold plugs are used in engines where the combustion chamber reaches very high temperatures: for example, a racing or high compression engine. Hot plugs are for more normal situations, such as a standard road engine where the compression ratio is not too high and the combustion chamber runs at a lower temperature. If, for example, you use a hot plug in a competition engine it is liable to burn and even melt the electrode; and if you put a cold plug in a standard engine you will get starting problems caused by the plug constantly fouling up. So it is very important to get it just right. The model numbers on the side of each spark plug will tell you the heat range and the reach (see Appendix for details).

By examining the spark plugs you can find out many problems occurring in the engine, whether it is a problem in just one cylinder or an overall engine problem – just looking at the plugs will give you a lot of information. If you are experiencing a problem with your engine at a certain rev range, then always look at the plugs after the engine has been running at this specific range; so if you are getting rough running at 4,000rpm, run the engine at this speed for a while, then switch off and check the plugs straightaway. Always remember that everything is going to be extremely hot now, so take great care; even when the plugs are out of the engine they will retain their heat for quite a while. Always examine each plug individually so that you know exactly which cylinder it has been taken from.

Figure 72 consists of a selection of spark-plug pictures showing various signs to look for; alongside are the explanations of the possible causes and cures.

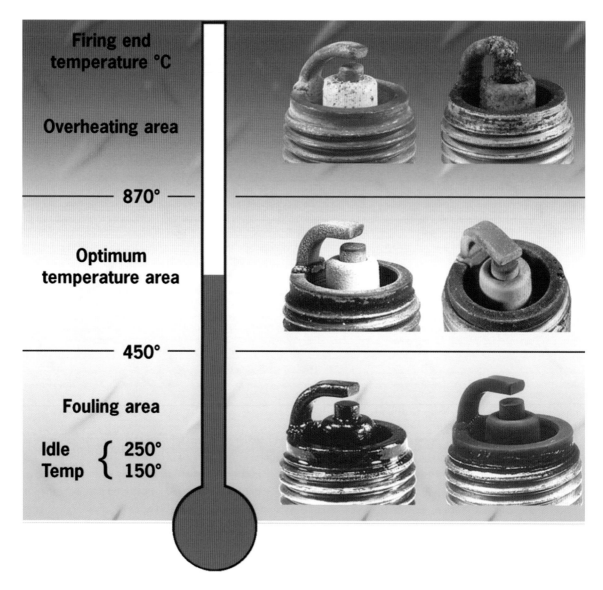

Fig. 72: A selection of spark-plug pictures showing various signs to look for; alongside are the explanations of the possible causes and cures. NGK

FAULT DIAGNOSIS OF SPARK-PLUG PROBLEMS

The majority of classic cars will run on either 14mm or 18mm spark plugs, so as well as the correct heat range you must have the correct thread diameter; also, the length of thread is extremely important, as too long and it could hit the piston, too short and it will not reach into the combustion chamber to obtain the best combustion. In the Appendix the various options for width and length of thread (the 'reach') are given, and the cross reference between Champion, NGK and Lodge.

Spark-plug manufacture has progressed over the years and it is possible to replace the original recommended plugs with a better modern alternative. For example, for the original Champion

- **Overheating**
The insulator is white and sometimes blistered. If the insulator temperature is over 870°C pre-ignition may occur. Engine power will be reduced and the piston may be damaged.

- **Causes**
- Over advanced ignition timing
- Too lean a fuel mixture
- Blocked injectors
- Insufficient cooling
- Excessive deposits in the combustion chamber

- **Good condition**
The insulator is brown or light grey.

Even if the spark plug is used under good conditions, deposits will accumulate. Regular inspection and replacement is advisable.

- **Fouling**
Carbon accumulates on the insulator nose forming a leakage path to earth. The engine misfires resulting in bad starting and poor acceleration. Particularly common with unleaded fuel.

- **Causes**
- Too rich a fuel mixture
- Excessive use of choke
- Prolonged slow speed driving or idling
- Blocked air filter
- Spark plug heat range too cold

N9Y you would now buy an N9YC, which is the copper-cored version; alternatively you could use the NGK BP6ES. With the information provided above you should now be able to make a good, safe choice for your engine. If you need advice, or you are finding it difficult to obtain the correct spark plugs, then The Green Spark Plug Company are the experts: with a wealth of knowledge and a massive selection of stock, this is the best company to contact.

Later in the book we will explain more about alternative plug choices when you are modifying your engine.

IGNITION LEADS

When dealing with the ignition system on a classic car, there is a good chance that the ignition leads are the same set that was fitted when the car was made. Most British classic cars used 7mm copper-cored ignition lead.

If you are going to replace the ignition leads it is possible in most cases to make them yourself, as the lead and all the terminals and plug caps are still available. If we look at the distributor cap side first, there are basically two types of fitting. The first is where there are acorn nuts that screw into the distributor cap to hold the wires in. On this system the insulation on the lead is stripped off to reveal about 10mm of the copper strands; these are then fed through the hole in a split copper washer and bent back to hold it on, *see* Fig. 48.

This then screws back into the distributor cap, making a contact and holding the lead tightly.

The second is as used on a 'push-fitting' cap. Here a specific terminal end is crimped on to the cable, though to do this correctly you need a special tool, as shown in Fig. 49. Once a good crimp is made, the wire then just pushes into the cap with the terminal cover making a nice tight, waterproof seal.

Fig. 73: A set of Magnecor ignition leads; these are their 7mm black ones, ideal for a standard classic car engine.

WHY AND WHEN SHOULD IGNITION LEADS BE REPLACED?
COURTESY OF PHIL DE WIT (MAGNECOR)

Ignition leads should be checked at regular intervals – that is, service intervals or every year if the annual mileage is low, to ascertain whether replacement is necessary. Visual checks should be made looking for signs of perishing or cuts and abrasion of the insulating jacket (the rubber covering over the core of the cable)/distributor and coil boots, and all connecting ends would need inspection for signs of corrosion at the connecting point or terminals, as they are called in the trade.

Each lead should also be checked with an ohm meter to ascertain whether the resistance of each lead is correct. There are different methods used by manufacturers to suppress ignition leads; for example, on classic cars a lot of leads were made using copper-core cable, which then screwed into a hard Bakelite resisted or suppressed sparkplug/distributor and/or coil cap. Hence when checking these leads you would generally look for equal resistance on all cables. If the resistance was not equal then further investigation would be warranted, looking for the cause of the inequality. This would usually be down to poor connections and resistor caps being open circuit.

Checking the dielectric strength (the insulating ability) of the cable's insulating jacket can prove difficult without special equipment. When the insulating jacket becomes unserviceable it usually shows up in damp weather, as it has a tendency to absorb moisture, which will then become conductive and the spark will jump to a suitable earth rather than across the spark-plug gap, or jump to another lead beside it and cause cross firing.

On leads that have rubber spark-plug boots rather than the hard Bakelite suppressed type the connecting terminals need to be examined for corrosion (if they are not stainless steel) and also for 'splayed' ends, due to being fitted and removed at incorrect angles, which will then cause the terminal to fit rather loosely: when under load this could result in a misfire.

When looking for a replacement set, especially for a classic car, you may want to retain originality, so do your homework before purchasing, as there are many brands of ignition lead of varying quality, and the wrong choice could prove unreliable. Seek out a specialist who can guide you in choices, and look for good quality silicone insulating jackets and high quality components to match, such as stainless steel terminals and silicone or EPDM rubber boots, especially at the spark-plug ends where the under-bonnet environment is harsh due to the heat. Nowadays even an MOT requires that the ignition leads have some sort of proof, as in 'printed on the cable', that they are in fact suppressed/resisted cables. This is because modern-day vehicles have many electronic devices on them that are prone to interference from erroneous signals from badly suppressed cables. In the early days when radios were introduced into vehicles, one of the biggest problems was the interference known as static; this was eradicated by dampening down the spark energy using resistors, which screwed into the ends of the cables.

Then there was the introduction of 'carbon-core' ignition leads, which had the same effect, by using a different method of suppression. Poor quality carbon-core leads have caused many problems over the years as a result of the carbon burning away leaving just the fibreglass stranding, which will not conduct.

While the standard ignition systems of classic cars have always proved capable of doing their job, the introduction of electronic ignition systems, which are more accurate and have fewer moving parts and are therefore prone to less wear and tear, has proved very popular, especially with classic cars. However, because electronic systems are more powerful and run using higher amperages, ignition leads are under more scrutiny as to their ability to cope with the higher voltages.

Classic cars also have some primitive methods of connecting to distributor caps and coils, hence the likelihood of a bespoke ignition lead kit needing to be made, in order to accommodate the later type of hardware.

Companies such as Magnecor can supply top quality, readymade sets of ignition leads. These are available in standard 7mm black or in a range of high performance alternatives.

Remember that when changing a set of ignition leads it is always advisable to change them one at a time so that you don't get confused as to which one goes where.

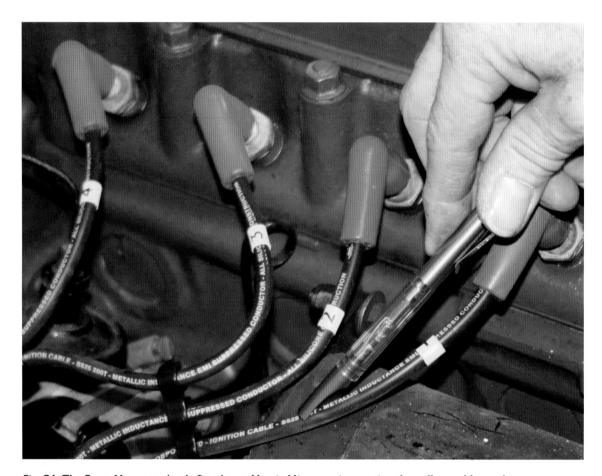

Fig. 74: The 7mm Magnecor leads fitted to a Morris Minor engine; notice the yellow cable markers.

CHAPTER FOUR

FAULT FINDING

NB: Please note that this chapter refers to negative-earth vehicles, unless otherwise stated.

Before starting any testing on ignition systems you must be aware that all ignitions circuits produce high voltages that can be dangerous; therefore always use insulated tools.

NOT STARTING

If the car won't start, first look at all the components, checking that all the HT and LT connections are actually connected and that nothing has come adrift. Make sure that your battery is in good condition, and that it is topped up to the correct level; if not, top it up with distilled or de-ionized water. Check the level of charge with a hydrometer.

If necessary clean both the battery terminals and the battery clamps on the ends of the leads. Also, follow the battery earth lead to where it joins the chassis and make sure this connection is good and clean. Bad earths are often the cause of many ignition problems.

Check the condition of the distributor cap and rotor: if either or both have bad corrosion or are heavily burnt, replace with new ones where needed. Then remove the spark plugs, check and clean them, and set the gap as described on page 39 .

Check the contact set and again, clean and set the gap or replace if needed.

Next, take the coil lead out of the distributor and hold the terminal inside close to the engine block, approximately 5mm away. Make sure you are holding this with insulated pliers. Turn on the ignition and operate the starter. Look for a good regular spark: if there is, then the fault is elsewhere.

At this point you can check the condenser. It is not possible to test the condenser so swap it, now, for a new one and do this test again. If the spark is much improved, then it shows that the original con-denser was poor, so keep the new one. If you are not obtaining a spark with either condenser, then replace the coil and repeat the test.

TESTING THE VOLTAGE

For the next test you will need a voltmeter, as we now need to find out if there is voltage at the positive terminal of the coil. Take off the distributor cap, and with the car out of gear, manually turn the engine until the contact set is closed. If you cannot do this manually, turn the engine using the ignition key. First of all turn on the ignition and flick the contacts open (this can be done with an insulated screwdriver): you should see a healthy spark across them. Now connect your voltmeter between the positive terminal of the coil and the other side to earth. Turn on the ignition and read the voltage: it should show a good 12 volts, unless you have a ballast-resisted system, in which case it will only show 6 or 9 volts. If this voltage is achieved, then the supply to the coil is fine.

If you are not obtaining this voltage, check the connections on the wire from the coil to the ignition switch, including the control box (regulator) if you have one fitted, making sure the connections are strong and not loose. If you are running a ballast-resisted system, check the wires to and from the ballast resistor; you will also need to check the starting voltage. With the voltmeter still connected between the positive terminal and earth, connect a lead from the negative coil terminal to earth (do not disconnect any of the original wiring). Turn the ignition on and crank the engine: while you are doing this the voltmeter should show full battery voltage.

If there is still a problem the next step is to test the voltage on the negative side of the coil. This time you need the contacts open. Connect the voltmeter between the negative coil terminal and earth, switch on the ignition and read the voltage: it should be battery voltage (at least 12 volts). Now disconnect the low tension lead to the distributor:

if the voltmeter still shows full battery voltage there is a short to earth in the distributor. Check the distributor and correct this. If the voltmeter does not show a voltage, then there may be a fault in the primary circuit of the coil.

Reconnect the low tension lead and leave the voltmeter connected. This time make sure that the contacts are closed. Switch the ignition on and read the voltage again: now it should read 0 volts. If it registers a voltage you must check all the earths, check that the contact set is in good condition and that the gap is correct, that the internal wirings in the distributor are in good order, and that the connections between the coil and distributor are clean and tight.

TESTING THE COIL

To test the coil, connect a voltmeter between the +ve terminal (SW) of the coil and a good earth – see Fig. 75 (negative earth instructions). With the contact points closed, switch on the ignition. Battery voltage should be registered, or if it is a ballast-resisted system, 6 volts. If there is a zero reading then there is an open circuit between the battery and the coil.

Now check the coil primary windings. Connect the voltmeter between a good earth and the –ve terminal (CB) of the coil – see Fig. 76. Battery voltage should be registered when the ignition is switched on and the contact points are open.

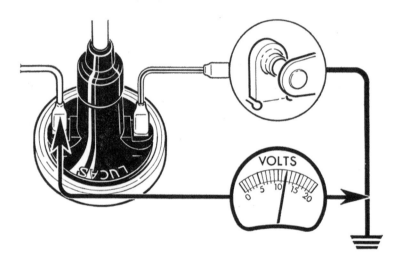

Fig. 75: Checking the supply voltage at the coil. LUCAS

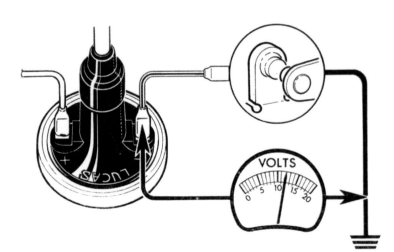

Fig. 76: Checking the primary windings. LUCAS

If the test shows the correct result, then connect the voltmeter between a good earth and the distributor LT terminal. With the ignition on and the contact points still open, the voltmeter should be reading battery voltage; if there is a zero reading, then there is either an open circuit in the primary winding of the coil, or there is a short circuit to earth in the coil to distributor LT lead or in the distributor.

To determine which of these it is, disconnect the lead from the coil −ve (CB) terminal. Leave the voltmeter still connected to this terminal, and with the ignition on, check the reading on the voltmeter. If it is zero then you have a faulty coil. If the voltmeter is showing battery voltage, then the coil is fine but there is an earth fault in the coil to distributor lead or in the distributor.

The rotor arm is the next part to be checked. Hold the HT lead that has been pulled out of the distributor cap close (about 3mm) to the rotor-arm electrode (blade): now flick the contacts open – there should not be a spark. If there is a spark, then there is a short through the rotor arm, in which case replace the arm with a new one, preferably a bonded type if available, not one with a blade that is riveted on.

If the engine will start but is just not running smoothly, then we need to look at some different things.

ROUGH RUNNING

Bad running can be caused by having a weak spark, or the spark is occurring at the wrong time.

First, check that your contact set and spark plugs are in good condition and that the gaps are correct. If the contact set is heavily pitted you may have a faulty condenser. A faulty condenser can also lead to the coil getting hot, but if this happens, also check *all* the earths in the ignition circuit.

The electrical current will always take the quickest route. More often these days, distributor caps and rotor arms are made from cheap inferior materials, and often they do not insulate the current well enough. The spark can then take a quicker path to the electrodes or cross between electrodes. This leaves a straight carbon mark and is called tracking, which can lead to bad running and misfiring. Look for any signs of tracking on the distributor cap and the rotor arm, and if you do find tracking marks, then replace the component with a good quality item. Certain companies – such as Retro Classic Car Parts Ltd – test all the options they can find and only supply the best ones available to provide the best reliability.

If the car's bad running is happening during damp weather, then it may be this damp that is causing the problems. After you have done the above checks, then spray the cap and the leads with something that expels damp, such as WD40, making sure that all the terminal end covers are sprayed.

CHAPTER FIVE

TIMING

Petrol engines operate on the principle of using a spark plug to ignite a compressed mixture of petrol and air in the cylinders of the engine. In practice, each spark plug fires slightly before a piston has reached the top of its compression stroke so that the petrol/air mixture has time to fully ignite before the commencement of the power stroke. The faster the engine is rotating, the greater is the angle before top dead centre (BTDC) that the spark plug has to fire.

Besides engine speed, the optimum timing of the spark depends on other factors, including the degree of suction in the inlet manifold (manifold vacuum), and whether leaded or unleaded petrol is being used. If the ignition timing of the engine is not correct, then either the performance or the economy of the engine will suffer, or both, and the engine exhaust will be high in hydrocarbons (HC) to a degree that might cause the vehicle to fail statutory exhaust emissions tests. If the spark happens too late the piston will be on its way back down the cylinder bore when the maximum expansion of the gases occurs. This results in a lower pressure exerted on the top of the piston and a resulting lack of power. Also, the

gases may still be burning when the exhaust valve opens, which can cause overheating and at worst can burn the exhaust valve.

If the spark happens too early, the maximum expansion of the gases will be before the piston reaches the end of the compression stoke, causing detonation. This will be very noticeable when the engine is under load. People commonly refer to this as 'pinking', and it can have very bad results, because if the 'pinking' progresses for too long or becomes 'heavier', it can result in burning the piston.

Many manufacturers continue to provide data on ignition timing; they also provide timing marks on the engine so the timing can be measured using a timing light, and some means by which the timing can be adjusted. Usually the data are provided at a particular engine idle RPM (the handbook usually also states whether the vacuum pipe should be connected or disconnected). This is generally referred to as 'static' timing. There are often corresponding timing marks on the fan-belt pulley or engine flywheel ('static timing marks') – see Fig. 77. Such ignition systems are designed so that if the user sets the 'static' timing

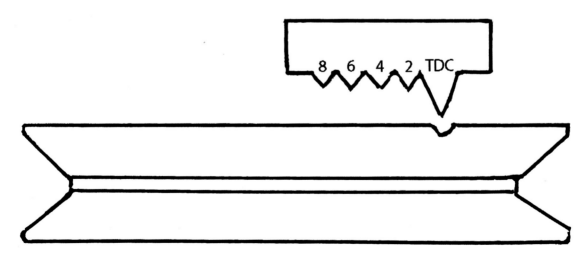

Fig. 77: A fan-belt pulley and a timing mark indicator. Notice the notch in the pulley: this marks the position to which the timing is adjusted.

correctly, then the automatic advance mechanisms will take over.

You will need to establish top dead centre (TDC): this is when piston number one is at its furthest distance from the crankshaft – that is, at its highest point in the combustion chamber. This is often marked on the crankshaft pulley along with other markings, these being degrees before top dead centre.

Manufacturers also commonly provide a top dead centre (TDC) mark in addition to a 'static' timing mark. Some manufacturers provide a TDC mark and no 'static' timing mark.

Perversely, car manufacturers usually provide no timing marks for engine speeds other than idle, even though timing data may be given for other speeds in the workshop manual. It is in such situations that the Gunsons Supastrobe Professional is very useful, since it can be used to measure the degrees of advance of ignition timing with respect to static timing, or TDC (or with respect to any other timing marks), and hence can be used to check service data where no suitable timing marks are provided on the fan-belt pulley or flywheel.

USING A TIMING LIGHT

A timing light is a device that works on the strobo-scopic principle – that is, a rotating part of an engine is made to appear stationary by being illuminated by a brief flash of light that occurs once per revolution (or multiples of a revolution), at the same rate that the engine is rotating.

The particular part of the engine that is made to appear to be stationary when using a timing light is a timing mark (or marks) that the car manufacturer has put on some rotating part of the engine, such as the fan-belt pulley or the engine flywheel. There is also always a fixed mark on the engine, close by where the moving mark passes, which is used as a reference position for the moving mark.

NON-ADVANCE TIMING LIGHT

A timing light takes its cue from the spark plug of number one cylinder, and flashes each time that spark plug fires. A non-advance timing light fires at

exactly the same instant that the spark plug fires. The timing mark on the rotating part of the engine therefore appears to be stationary in exactly the position it has at the time of the spark to number one cylinder spark plug. From the apparent position of the moving mark in relation to the fixed mark, the timing of the engine can be determined. For example, if the rotating mark represents 8 degrees BTDC, and appears to be exactly opposite the fixed reference mark, then the ignition timing is 8 degrees BTDC.

This is fine if all the user wishes to do is check that the timing is 8 degrees BTDC. However, maybe the moving mark is not exactly opposite the fixed mark, and the user still wishes to know what the timing is. Maybe he wishes to set the timing to some value for which there is no timing mark. Or maybe he wishes to check the timing at higher RPM, for which the car manufacturer has provided data in the handbook, but has not provided timing marks on the fan-belt pulley. For these jobs a simple non-advance timing light is not adequate, and the user needs an advance timing light.

ADVANCE TIMING LIGHT

An advance timing light includes electronic circuitry that can apply a small but precise delay between the time the spark plug fires and the time that the timing light flashes. Delaying the flash of the timing light has the same effect on the apparent position of the timing marks as advancing the ignition timing by the same amount. This can be seen to be true by considering that, if two timing marks are brought into conjunction by delaying the timing light flash, then the actual spark from the spark plug must have occurred some time earlier. In the Gunson Supastrobe, as shown in Fig. 78, the time of the flash is controlled by the advance knob on the rear control panel of the instrument.

Rotating this knob fully anticlockwise applies no delay to the flash, and it behaves as an ordinary, non-advance timing light (the display shows 00.00). However, rotating the knob clockwise causes the flash of the timing light to be delayed by the angle shown on the display: that is, the angle shown on

Fig. 78: The Gunson Supastrobe: the ideal inductive timing light.

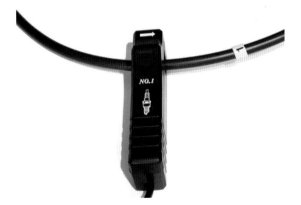

the display needs to be added to whatever advance angle is being indicated by the timing marks on the engine.

This particular timing light is known as an inductive timing light, and it comes with a slide-type sensor that fits over the number one plug lead and senses the pulses (see Fig. 79).

Fig. 79: The Gunson inductive pick-up shown on lead no. 1.

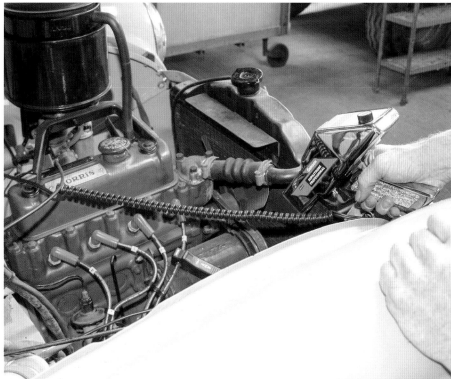

Figs 80 & 81: At the top is the inductive pick-up on the number one lead; on the bottom is the timing being checked.

To illustrate this, consider the example mentioned above, of a 'static' timing mark on a fan-belt pulley representing 8 degrees BTDC. This mark would still represent 8 degrees BTDC if the display on the timing light were 00.00, but it would represent 28 degrees BTDC if the knob were rotated to show 20.00 on the display.

The use of this timing light is particularly simple where the engine timing marks have an indication for top dead centre (TDC), which many engines have. Using the TDC marks, the ignition timing is simply as shown on the rear panel display of the timing light. For example, if the TDC mark is opposite the fixed mark when the display shows 00.00, then the timing is TDC, but if the display shows 08.00, then the ignition timing is 8 degrees BTDC, and if the display shows 20.00, then the ignition timing is 20 degrees BTDC.

Don't forget to retighten the clamp, though make sure not to over-tighten it, as this can damage the distributor. Fig. 82 shows a typical distributor that has been over-tightened – but if this happens, don't worry: this is not the end of your distributor, and it can be fixed.

Setting the correct ignition timing is best done at normal operating temperature. Loosen the pinch bolt on the distributor clamp, so that it can turn freely. If your distributor has a vacuum unit fitted, remove the vacuum hose. Copper vacuum pipes will probably need to be unscrewed whereas the later rubber pipes can just be pulled off. On most British engines the rotor arm rotates anticlockwise, so to advance the ignition timing you need to rotate the distributor body clockwise. If you have an engine where the rotor arm rotates in a clockwise direction, then turn the distributor body anti-clockwise.

Once the correct timing is achieved, this should be checked with the timing light, then tighten the distributor clamp bolt and refit the vacuum hose.

ADVANCE CURVES

As mentioned earlier in the book, a distributor that is fitted with weights and springs creates an advance curve when running from zero to maximum revs. These advance curves are tailored to the individual engine into which the distributor is being fitted. This is one reason why, although two distributors look absolutely identical, they are in fact totally different, and the one should never replace the other. Fitting a distributor with the wrong advance curve will not just cause bad or inefficient running: it could have disastrous effects. If you have a distributor that uses only 10 degrees maximum advance and you fit a distributor that has 20 degrees, the engine will over-advance and at worst could blow up.

Figure 83 shows a typical advance curve graph, in this case for the Lucas 40510 as used on the MGA. The two lines show the upper and lower limits of the advance curve, as you will see in the figures given below.

Fig. 82: The damage caused by over-tightening a distributor clamp.

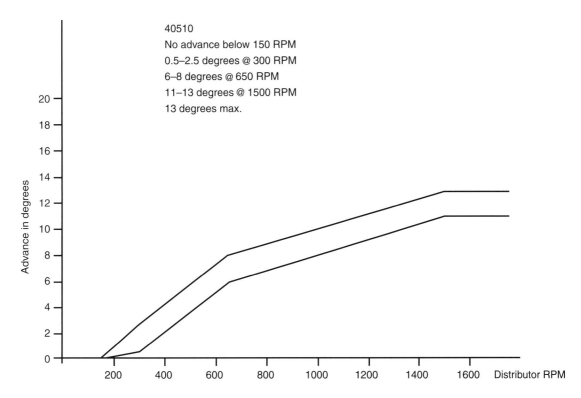

40510
No advance below 150 RPM
0.5–2.5 degrees @ 300 RPM
6–8 degrees @ 650 RPM
11–13 degrees @ 1500 RPM
13 degrees max.

Fig. 83: Graph representing the advance curve for the Lucas 40510, the MGA distributor.

The original specifications for this would be given as:

Run up to 1,500rpm
Advance in degrees 11–13
Rev/min 650
Advance in degrees 6–8
Rev/min 300
Advance in degrees 0.5–2.5
No advance below 150

You will notice that advance curves, when written, are always shown from the maximum advance and at what speed this occurs, then drop to the point where there is no advance. This is because when setting an advance curve the distributor is run up to speed and then set with the speed decreasing. There will always be an accurate speed setting, but there is usually a tolerance of 2 degrees for the advance figure – that is, 6–8 degrees @ 650rpm.

A SELECTION OF POPULAR CLASSIC CAR ADVANCE CURVES

The table shows the original specifications for a range of popular classic cars. It must be noted that these figures are distributor figures and not engine figures, so when you are timing your 3.8 E-type Jaguar engine, don't panic when the advance goes way above 12 degrees. To calculate engine figures you must double these figures and add whatever the static timing is of the engine: this is because distributors rotate at half engine speed – that is, if your distributor gives a maximum of 12 degrees and your static timing is 8 degrees, then the calculation is 2×12+8=32 degrees, and this will be the figure you should expect to see when you check the advance of your engine (tested with the vacuum disconnected).

Classic Car Advance Curves

Application	Distributor Number	Vac. Code	Run up to (RPM)	Advance degrees	RPM	Advance degrees	RPM	Advance degrees	No advance below
Aston Martin DB6	41083	No Vacuum	1500	8–10	750	4.5–6.5	500	1–3	275
Austin Healey 3000 BJ8	40966	5–12–8	3200	17–19	850	6.5–8.5	550	1–4	300
Ford Anglia – Cortina	40857	5–17–10	3000	12.5–14.5	1500	8–10	700	0.5–3	575
MGA	40510	7–14–10	1500	11–13	650	6–8	300	0.5–2.5	150
MGB 1969–1974	41288	5–13–10	1500	9–11	800	6.5–8.5	300	0–3	200
Jaguar E-type 3.8	40887	7–14–8	2000	12max	850	7–9	450	0–2.5	250
Jaguar E-type 4.2	41060	7–14–8	2300	8.5–10.5	800	5–7	525	0–1.5	300
Land Rover 1956–59	40504	7–18–12	3100	20–22	1250	6–8	750	0–1	600
Mini Cooper S	40819	No vacuum	3800	14–16	800	5–7	300	0–1.5	225
Triumph TR4	40795	2–6–3	1200	9–11	600	5–7	350	0–2	225

CHAPTER SIX

MODIFICATION AND COMPETITION

Many people spend thousands of pounds modifying their engines, increasing the capacity, fitting high-lift camshafts and larger carburettors. On many occasions they then totally ignore the distributor and ignition system. But unless you get your distributor matched to your engine you are not going to achieve the maximum performance available.

There are many modifications that can be done to the ignition system, but let's start with the most important: the distributor. In most cases, to achieve maximum performance you have to sacrifice other criteria. For example if you are after ultimate power you are going to lose fuel economy and smoothness at low speeds. The standard setting for a car's distributor will be to achieve smooth running and economy, but to make it match a modified engine these two things will not be a priority.

REPLACEMENT DISTRIBUTORS

Although many replacement modified distributors are now available 'off the shelf', be very careful in buying one, and only go to a true specialist such as H & H Ignition Solutions: they will be able to supply a whole range of conventional points-type or electronic distributors to suit a whole variety of engines. Once again, beware of the 'cheap bargains' that you will frequently see advertised. Figure 84 shows the H & H Ignition electronic distributor they have for the Ford Pinto (ohc) engine, a highly respected unit that is a good upgrade for the standard Bosch or Motorcraft points distributors. These can be bought with or without a vacuum unit and to suit various stages of tune.

For the Ford X-flow engines there is the Lucas competition department constant energy distributor kit, as shown in Fig. 85. This unit also suits Lotus twin-cam and Cosworth BDA derivatives and, like the Pinto Bosch unit, is available to suit various stages of engine tune right up to full race engines.

Fig. 84: The H & H Ignition electronic distributor to fit the Ford SOHC engine.

A good modified distributor will get you quite close to where you need to be, but for things to be 100 per cent perfect, have the distributor set as part of a rolling-road tune-up – though make sure you go to a reputable rolling road with competition experience, because some rolling roads will not alter the distributor. When fitting a modified distributor to a modified engine you will find that for best results you may need to use a different static timing setting, depending on the number and type of modifications

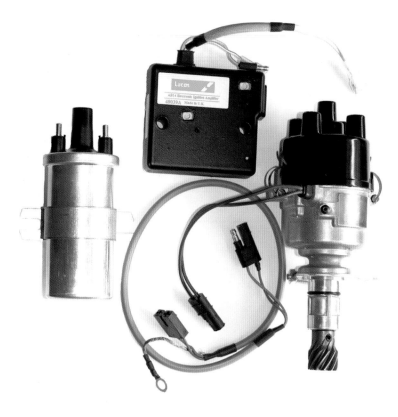

Fig. 85: The Lucas Constant Energy 43D4 kit.

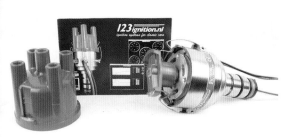

Fig. 86: The '123 Tune' totally programmable distributor.

that you have done. The most important here is if you have changed to a much higher lift camshaft, especially one that has a lot of overlap, as using these types of camshaft means you will have to increase the static timing to suit.

Another alternative and a real technical leap forward are the 123 Ignition distributors, as shown in Fig. 86. The version shown is the replacement for the Lucas 4-cylinder distributors such as the 25D4 and the 45D4.

These units are programmable! They were made with sixteen pre-set advance curves that the customer could choose to suit his engine, but at the time of writing we were able to obtain the 123 Tune, their brand new model. This unit can be used to replace distributors that rotate clockwise or anticlockwise, 6 volt or 12 volt and positive earth or negative earth – and it doesn't stop there! Each unit connects to a laptop via a USB cable and is totally programmable. You can set two individual advance curves (for example, for when a car is using two different fuels), two vacuum curves and two rev limiters, and it also has variable dwell.

On loading the software on to a laptop you are presented with a 'dashboard' showing five gauges and a 'settings' page where you see two graphs. Once you connect the new distributor you can then programme the unit with the information required – and once the distributor is fitted back in the car there is still more you can do! For example, if the car is on a rolling road, you can plug in the laptop and reprogram the distributor while the engine is running to obtain maximum power throughout the rev range – a fantastic feature for competition cars. And if this is not enough, it also has an RPM stopwatch facility.

Quite apart from all these fantastic facilities, these make great replacements for old standard distributors; but it would be advisable to ask your supplier to set the distributor to the correct specification for your car if you don't have access to this information.

REPLACEMENT V8 DISTRIBUTORS

There were four different Lucas distributors that were based around the 35D8, the 'Rover V8' distributor:

- The 35D8: the standard points-type distributor fitted to the Rover V8, Rolls-Royce V8 and a twin-point version on the Triumph Stag
- The 35DE8: an Opus electronic distributor
- The 35DM8: a constant energy system with a separate ignition amplifier fitted remotely
- The 35DLM8: also a constant energy system but with the amplifier fitted to the side of the distributor body

As mentioned, these distributors were fitted to a variety of engines, but all of them can be replaced by a new constant energy kit designed and made by H

Fig. 87: The 35DLM8-based electronic ignition kit for the Aston Martin V8.

& H Ignition Solutions, based on the Lucas 35DLM8. Figure 87 shows the Aston Martin V8 version, complete with the Lucas DLB198 coil.

UPRATED COILS

To cope with the modifications made to the engine, especially if it is now free to rev higher, it is a good idea to fit a better coil to replace the standard one fitted. A standard coil only produces in the region of 17kv, whereas upgrading to a sports coil can give you in the region of 30kv or even more.

When fitting an uprated coil to a conventional points ignition system you need a sports coil, but make sure it is not an electronic type coil. A standard sports coil such as the Lucas DLB105 or the Bosch Blue Sports Coil as shown in Fig. 88 are ideal units, and they are just direct replacements. These coils produce more secondary voltage and rejuvenate themselves much more quickly than a standard coil, enabling engine speeds of up to about 8,000rpm.

Another sports coil that can be a great alternative is the Pertronix Flame Thrower, as shown in

Fig. 88: Lucas DLB105 and the Bosch Blue sports coils.

Fig. 89: The Pertronix Flame Thrower with a 40,000 volt coil.

Fig. 89: these can achieve up to 40,000 volts. These perform extremely well in all non-ballast-resisted 12-volt systems that require a 3ohm coil, whether it is a points distributor or if you are using electronic ignition (not the high energy systems that require a modern electronic coil). With these coils you will be able to increase the spark-plug gap to achieve greater fuel economy and more power. An ideal partner for this would be the Pertronix Ignitor.

One point to note is that both the Bosch Blue sports coil and the Pertronix Flame Thrower do not come with a coil bracket, so you may have to use your old one or purchase one separately.

SPARK PLUGS

When the ignition system has been uprated to suit the needs of a competition or high performance engine, it is also necessary to fit suitable spark plugs. When using electronic ignition on modified engines it is usually beneficial to choose a 'colder' spark plug as it conducts heat more quickly to the combustion chamber than a hot plug, thus lowering the temperature of the spark-plug tip. The hot plug, however, is better insulated and keeps more heat in. *See pages 89–92 for details on spark-plug heat ranges.*

CHAPTER SEVEN

ELECTRONIC IGNITION

There are many types of electronic ignition kit available for many classic applications.

LUMENITION ELECTRONIC IGNITION KITS

Autocar Ltd have been making Lumenition electronic ignition kits with great success since the 1960s, while I have personally used these kits for thirty years without a fault.

Autocar have been a UK-based manufacturer and distributor of automotive electronics since 1922, when the current managing director, Mr Michael Ford's grandfather, started an automobile garage. Michael Ford's father, Eric Ford, inherited the growing business and expanded its activities to become distributors for Briggs and Stratton engines, Hirschman, Pioneer, Alpine and Autolite (as sole UK distributor) and other companies based in the UK, Europe, Japan and the USA.

They have three types available: Magnetronic, a compact Hall Effect system that fits entirely inside the distributor; Standard Optronic, the famous infra-red system, which has an external power pack; and Performance Optronic, which comes with a special coil and has variable dwell.

The first optical ignition system was created in 1967, with the Optronic patent applied for in February 1968 and granted a year later. In October 1968 it was showcased at the London Motor Show, and later was presented on the television programme *Tomorrow's World*, when Eric Ford demonstrated the product to Raymond Baxter (*see* Fig. 90).

THE LUMENITION OPTRONIC SYSTEM

In 1971 the world's first optical ignition was launched, the Lumenition Optronic system; it has been in constant production ever since, and in 1974 it was granted a Queen's Award for Industry and won a Design Council award.

Having just enjoyed its fortieth anniversary (at the time of writing), the system effectively created a third party electronic contact-breaker replacement market, achieving unparalleled success with over 500,000 units sold worldwide. Despite cheaper competitor products coming to the market, including rebadged imports from the Far East, the Lumenition Optronic still retains a major share of the UK and worldwide market despite its higher price, and has a well deserved reputation for being long-lived and reliable in operation.

The Optronic is a non-destructive fitment for 95 per cent of the thousand makes and models of vehicles it has been designed for. This means that should there be a problem with the system, for whatever reason, it is always possible to re-fit the points and condenser and continue your journey.

The current Mk17 version of the standard Optronic has been in production since 1986, and all units manufactured since that time have component parts available for the power module and optical switch (see Fig. 91).

FITTING AN OPTRONIC KIT

Below is a step-by-step guide to fitting an Optronic kit, in this case to a Lucas DM2 distributor. The great thing about fitting an Optronic unit is that it has no wearing parts and requires no adjustment or maintenance – so it really is a question of 'fit it and forget it'. The basic system consists of three parts:

- The optical switch: this contains a light-emitting diode (LED), which sits in the switch bracket opposite a matching silicon phototransistor. When the ignition is on, the LED emits an invisible infra-red beam towards the silicon transistor, which receives the beam

Fig. 90: Eric Ford and Raymond Baxter in 1968 on Tomorrow's World.

Fig. 91: A Lumenition Optronic kit
PMA50.

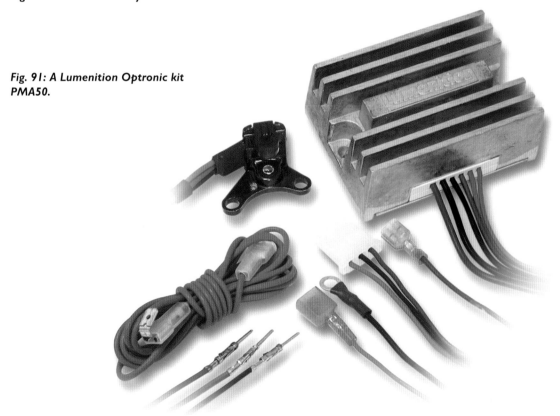

Fig. 92: Lumenition Optronic power pack fitted on the inner wing of a Morris Minor.

- The chopper blade: this sits over the distributor cam, which, as it rotates, interrupts the beam of light causing a pulse
- The external power module: this receives the pulse via its internal electronic device, which switches the ignition coil on and off. The coil produces a high tension spark when switched off, and is recharged when switched on

This system is suitable to use with all coils or coil/ballast combinations of not less than 3ohm, but must not be used with low resistance electronic coils (less than 1ohm).

First of all you need to disconnect the battery earth lead, and then find a suitable place to fit the power pack, not too far away from the distributor and not too close to the exhaust (see Fig. 92). It is recommended that if you are fitting this to a fibreglass body, then you should run an earth lead direct from the mounting screw to the battery earth terminal.

Connect the red wire (using the extension wire supplied if needed) to either:

- The feed side of the ignition terminal on the fuse box

- The ignition switch side of the ballast resistor, not the coil side
- The ignition terminal of the ignition switch – but do not connect to the auxiliary terminals, which switch off in start or cranking position

Connect the brown wire (this is violet on later units) to the wire from which the contact breaker was removed. This goes to the negative terminal on the coil (on negative earth cars).

Fitting the Optical Switch

For ease we removed the distributor to fit the optical switch, but this can be done with the distributor still fitted as long as it is totally accessible (see Fig. 93).

- Remove the contact set, condenser and LT lead from the distributor. It is important to the operation of the unit that the earth strap is re-attached to the base plate. The Lumenition fitting kit will be supplied with any necessary adaptor plates to suit the individual distributor
- Fit the optical eye to the base plate with the screws provided. Run the wires from the optical eye around the inside edge of the distributor body, securing them to the base

Fig. 93: The Optical eye and the chopper blade fitted to a distributor.

plate with the small tie-wrap provided. These then exit the body through the original LT lead hole using the grommet provided

- Fit the chopper blade over the cam, making sure that it does not come into contact with the leads when the cam is turned. It is also advisable to check that the wires do not interfere with any movement of the vacuum unit
- Re-fit the rotor arm and cap
- On the end of the three wires are three contact pins: ensure that the 'tags' on these pins are opened out slightly so that they locate and lock into the connector block. Give the wires a slight pull to check that they have located correctly
- When fitting the plug connector to the three wires coming from the optical eye, it is critical to get them in the right order. This can be checked when connecting this plug to the corresponding plug from the power pack: ensure that the colours of the wires match on either side

- Re-fit the distributor, if removed, and check the timing. Make sure that the distributor is now set to the manufacturer's specifications
- Use a voltmeter between the ignition coil negative terminal and earth. Turn the engine and align the correct timing marks, ensuring that the rotor arm is pointing to the correct distributor cap terminal – this is normally number one
- With the distributor cap removed, the leading edge of the chopper blade should be two-thirds across the optical eye lens in the direction of rotation. Slacken off the distributor clamp bolt and slightly turn the distributor so that the chopper blade is just before the point of passing past the optical eye. Now, switch on the ignition
- Very gently turn the distributor against the direction of rotation to the exact point where the voltmeter reads 12 volts. When correct, tighten the clam, remove the voltmeter and replace the distributor cap. The engine should now be ready to start

When fitting a Lumeniton kit I always recommend fitting a new rotor arm and cap.

FAULT FINDING

If the unit is not working, here are some tests that will help you find and eliminate the problem. All of these are done with the ignition switched on and the centre HT lead removed and held approximately 65mm from a good earth point such as the engine block – but be sure to keep well away from the carburettor's fuel supply.

- With the distributor cap removed, pass a piece of opaque material such as card between the lenses of the optical switch; you should notice a spark from the HT lead to earth
- Unplug the connector block leading to the distributor, and connect the blue and the black wires that lead to the power module; this can be done with the aid of a small piece of wire. As these are connected you should see a spark from the HT lead. If there is no spark the power module may be at fault, but if there is a weak spark then the coil may be at fault
- If you have done the above test and find no fault with the power module, then it is time to test the optical switch. With the use of a volt-meter, measure the voltage between the blue and the black wires. When the light beam is not interrupted the voltage should be approximately 2.7 volts; this will drop to about 1 volt when the beam is interrupted. The voltage on the red wire should show 7.5 volts

If the Optronic system is to be used on a positive earth car than you need to adhere strictly to the following instructions: failure to do this will lead to damage.

- Remove the original ignition lead from the coil negative terminal
- The black wire from the module should not be fitted under the mounting screw, but instead should be connected to the ignition switch feed. This is usually the wire removed from the coil
- The red wire from the module can be connected to the chassis or positive earth
- The violet wire (newer units) or the brown wire (older units) from the module should be connected to the coil negative terminal
- The positive terminal on the coil must be connected to the chassis of vehicle positive earth using an extra wire. If there is a ballast resistor it should be wired between this terminal and the vehicle earth

THE MAGNETRONIC UNIT

This is a great unit for use on classic cars. Not visible under the bonnet, and with no external power pack, this unit fits entirely inside the distributor; the only clue that electronic ignition is fitted are the two wires coming from the distributor and going to the coil. This is a 'Hall Effect' unit, where a small module is mounted to the distributor base plate and a timing disc is fitted over the distributor cam, just under the rotor arm.

There are several other electronic ignition kits that work in a similar way, but lots of them have the timing rotor parallel to the module, and in this situation, any play in the distributor shaft can cause the timing rotor to come in contact with the module, with devastating results. The Magnetronic has the timing rotor in the same plane as the module directly above it, and in this case if there is any play in the distributor shaft there can be no contact, and hence no problems. At the time of writing Magnetronic kits are available for certain Lucas distributors and certain Bosch units, but all must be negative earth (see Fig. 94).

FITTING THE MAGNETRONIC UNIT

The Magnetronic unit is very easy to fit, but is only suitable for negative earth cars:

- Disconnect the battery
- Remove the distributor cap, rotor, contact set and condenser. Make sure that the earth lead

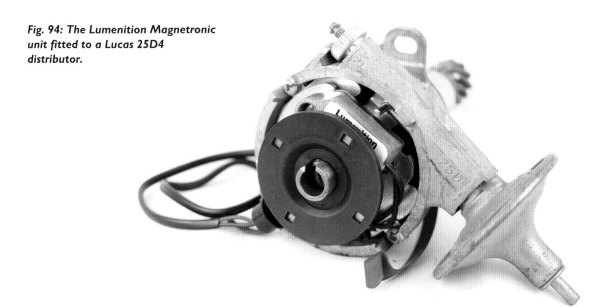

Fig. 94: The Lumenition Magnetronic unit fitted to a Lucas 25D4 distributor.

connecting the distributor base plates is re-attached

- Fit the adaptor plate supplied by locating the flattened hole over the pivot pin, and secure with the screw supplied. Some pivot pins will need to be shortened to the same height as the adaptor plate
- Fit the Magnetronic module to the adaptor plate, and secure with the screw and washer provided
- Feed the wires around the inside of the distributor body, allowing sufficient slack for the advance mechanism to move and ensuring that the wires are not close to any moving parts
- Feed the wire out of the distributor body through the supplied grommet
- Fit the magnetic disc over the cam; the lobes of the cam fit between the ribs in the disc. Ensure that the disc is seated firmly
- The distance between the underside of the disc and the top of the module should be approximately 1.5mm
- Fit the spade connectors to the module wires
- Connect the red wire to the ignition-feed coil terminal. If a ballast resistor is fitted the red wire must be connected to the ignition switch side of the resistor. Connect the black

wire to the negative coil terminal. This is the terminal to which the contact breaker was originally connected. Discard the original wire connected to the condenser
- Refit the rotor arm and cap
- Check the engine timing

FAULT FINDING

- If there is no spark from the coil when cranking the engine, switch on the ignition and check for 12 volts on the red wire for the module
- Check the terminals on the red and black wires to verify that they are crimped properly and attached to the correct terminals
- With the ignition switched off, remove the distributor cap and check the air gap between the module and the magnetic disc: it should be approximately 1.5mm and must be between 0.75mm and 2.55mm
- If all this is correct you must test the module
- Make sure that the transmission is in neutral and the hand brake is on
- Disconnect the tachometer sense lead from the coil if there is one fitted
- Set a voltmeter to DC with a range of between 15 and 60 volts

- Connect the positive meter lead to the negative coil terminal
- Connect the negative meter lead to earth
- Crank the engine

If the needle jumps back and forth between approximately 1 and 13 volts, the ignition system is working properly and the problem is elsewhere in the system, perhaps the coil, leads or rotor. If the needle stays at 13 volts, either the red or the black wire is not making a good connection to the coil. If the needle stays at 1 volt, there may be an excessive air gap between the module and the magnetic rotor, or the module has been damaged by connecting the red and black wires to the wrong terminals on the coil.

THE LUMENITION PERFORMANCE KIT

In 1991 Lumenition released the 'Performance' kit, still an optical system but with extra features. This has a different power module, which calculates the coil dwell angle depending on the RPM and number of cylinders. This kit is also supplied with a 1 ohm constant energy electronic coil to match. The microcircuit control of this coil gives optimum performance across the whole speed and voltage range, ensuring constant maximum spark energy at the coil.

This also has variable dwell angle, which optimizes energy to prevent low speed coil overheat. There is also an automatic switch-off, preventing electrical damage in the event of the ignition being left on.

This is a great system for competition cars, as it can deal with the high-revving engines that are needed.

THE PERTRONIX IGNITOR

Founded in 1962, Pertronix was originally known as Per-Lux, a company that made lighting equipment. In the early 1970s they came up with the idea of an electronic ignition system that would replace the points and condenser in distributors – and so the Ignitor was born. They changed their name in 1991 to 'PerTronix' and totally committed themselves to the ignition business.

The Ignitor is a solid-state Hall Effect electronic ignition system that replaces the points and condenser and fits entirely inside the distributor cap; the only thing you see are two wires coming out of the distributor and connecting to the ignition coil. This produces twice the voltage of the standard points and condenser system, and increases horsepower, fuel economy and the life of the spark plugs. An ideal partner for this is the Pertronix Flame Thrower coil. The photograph in Fig. 95 shows an Ignitor fitted to a Jaguar XCK150 distributor; this was actually fitted

Fig. 95: A Lucas DMBZ6A fitted with an Ignitor unit.

Fig. 96: The Ignitor II with the matching Flame Thrower II.

without removing the distributor, but we removed it for illustration purposes.

On fitting the Ignitor there was an improvement in starting and the XK150 engine was even smoother!

THE IGNITOR II AND III

Since the advent of the famous Ignitor there has been another leap forwards: the Ignitor II (see Fig. 96). Although this may look very similar it is much more advanced. The Ignitor II units sense the coil current level and use a powerful micro-controller to adjust the dwell. Variable dwell helps to maintain peak energy throughout the entire rpm range, which will reduce any misfiring and improve the engine performance. This unit develops four times the available energy between 3,000 and 5,000rpm, and twice the available plug voltage.

This system needs to be partnered with a low-resistance coil, and the Flame Thrower II is ideal: this ignition coil is a 0.6 ohm unit and produces 45,000 volts. This higher voltage enables you to run larger spark-plug gaps for added power and better fuel economy. With this system you should not use solid copper-core spark plug leads: a suppression style or spiral-wound spark-plug lead must be used. Pertronix make suitable spark-plug leads to match.

If you are looking for absolute performance there is also the Ignitor III, which is claimed to have five times more spark energy than a standard points system. The Ignitor III has an integrated rev limiter, which is adjustable between 4,000 and 9,000rpm. It features adaptive dwell, which maintains peak energy throughout the entire rpm range, reducing misfires while improving engine performance. Peak current level is reached just prior to spark for maximum energy without the heat build-up, increasing coil performance and module reliability. The Ignitor III adjusts spark timing at higher revs to compensate for the inherent electronic delay, senses start-up, and develops more energy for quicker, easier starting. There is also built-in reverse polarity, and over-current protection shuts down the system. This unit needs to be paired with the Flame Thrower III ignition coil, an ultra low-resistance (0.32-ohm) 45,000-volt coil.

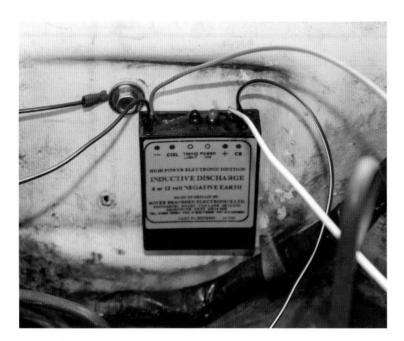

Fig. 97: The Boyer-Bransden electronic ignition kit.

BOYER-BRANSDEN

Boyer-Bransden is a famous name in the motorcycle community throughout the world. In 1969 their first electronic ignition was launched for Boyer of Bromley, a then famous motorcycle dealership whose Triumph race team was experiencing trouble with the points on their race bikes. It proved an instant success, and they had already sold over 2,000 units before Lucas introduced their Rita system. Now there is a Boyer-Bransden system available for cars.

The 'inductive discharge unit', which is inexpensive to buy and extremely simple to fit, is ideal for anyone wishing to improve the running of older, classic or high mileage cars with traditional coil and distributor ignition, 6 or 12 volts, positive or negative earth. Timing worries and sparking at the points are a thing of the past. Points life is extended beyond 30,000 miles, and more energy reaches the spark plug for improved combustion and mpg. Often the improvement in efficiency is made immediately apparent by an increase in idle speed. This can be corrected by simply turning down the idle adjustment on the carburettor. This system does not affect normal electronic rev counters.

The unit has only four wires, and if the function of each is understood, fitting can be simplified. The white wire feeds to the ignition unit, and this should become live when the ignition is switched on. The black wire is the earth wire for the ignition unit and connects to the chassis, and removes paint from its point of contact; one of the ignition coil mounting bolts is satisfactory. The blue wire carries the ignition coil current and connects to the negative or CB terminal on the ignition coil (the ballast resistor must be left in the circuit if fitted). The black/white wire carries a small current to the contact breaker.

On testing this unit we fitted it into a Triumph TR6 distributor in less than five minutes, and the difference was instant: it was running much more smoothly, and this could be noticed without even having a test drive!

SATEL ELECTRONIC SPARK

As soon as you take this unit out of the box you are aware that it is very solid and well made. These units come from Italy where they are made. It is enclosed in a water-tight, heavy duty plastic body

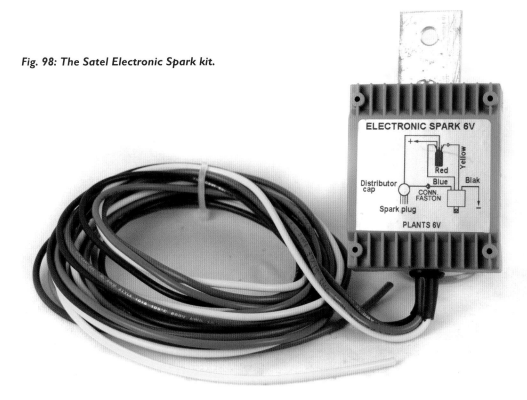

Fig. 98: The Satel Electronic Spark kit.

with a steel mounting bracket that has a single bolt hole for fitting. It is available for both 6-volt and 12-volt systems, and in each you have the choice of either positive or negative earth – so make sure you choose the right one.

The Satel Electronic Spark is designed to increase the efficiency of the ignition system while keeping the standard contact breaker points. The contact breaker points are now just used as a position sensor and are not passed by current, and because of this it doesn't matter if they are pitted or corroded. The condenser becomes redundant and can be removed or left fitted.

Along the lines of the Boyer-Bransden system, this unit is really easy to fit simply by connecting four wires. The black wire, no surprise, is the earth. The green wire attaches to the low tension wire coming from the distributor. The other two wires go to the coil: red to the positive side and yellow to the negative. Ample wire and all the terminals you will need are provided so that the unit can be discreetly mounted on the bulkhead or inner wing.

The primary current output is slightly lower than normal, but much steadier and more rapid. The system then as a whole is much more efficient and responsive, besides the fact that the discharge to the spark plugs is more powerful.

When fitted, the engine of the Morris Minor in which we tested it certainly seemed smoother, and starting was instant! If you don't want to change to totally contactless electronic ignition this unit is definitely a great alternative.

REV LIMITERS

After several modifications it is possible that an engine can rev so freely that it has to be limited to prevent it from blowing itself apart. Originally it would have been fitted with a rev-limiting rotor arm that shorted itself out when it reached the desired revs, and in fact these have been used as original equipment on cars until very recently. You will see in Fig. 99 that the number of revs at which it cuts out is stamped into the arm – though remember that the

Fig. 99: Lucas rev-limiter arm showing the 2,700rpm limit.

engine revs at twice this speed, so 3,250 will cut the engine at 6,500rpm.

Otherwise an electronic cut-out unit might be used, such as the Lumenition or Micro Dynamics rev limiters (see Fig. 100).

The Lumenition engine rev limiter (ERL) is designed to be used with inductive contact breaker and electronic ignition systems with fixed or variable dwell, with or without ballast resistors, and with standard or high energy ignition coils. The rev limiter functions by monitoring the voltage pulses at the coil negative terminal. When the engine speed reaches the set limit, the amplitude of the coil drive voltage is clipped and prevents sufficient secondary voltage being generated in the coil, thus inhibiting the firing of the spark plugs. As the engine speed drops the voltage limit is removed, and normal coil function resumes.

The limiting speed is pre-set during production at 5,500rpm on 4-cylinder operation. This speed may be either increased or decreased after installation to obtain a limiting speed within the ranges listed. The accuracy and stability of the speed setting selected will depend on the accuracy of the tachometer used for reading the engine speed. These are programmable to the desired rpm.

Fig. 100: Lumenition and Micro Dynamics rev limiters.

FITTING A LUMENITION ERL REV LIMITER

With the negative battery terminal removed, choose a flat mounting space, ideally next to the power module where the rev limiter can be mounted with the two fitting screws provided. However, remember that if you are mounting this on a fibreglass panel you must run a heavy duty earth wire from one of the mounting screws direct to the battery earth terminal. Connect the brown wire to the negative terminal of the coil, and the red wire to an ignition switch input to the fusebox, or an ignition-switched terminal that is not fused. The black lead goes to earth.

IDENTIFICATION OF DISTRIBUTORS AND SPARK PLUGS

Manufacturer-fitted distributors usually have either a model number or a part number, or both, stamped on the side of each unit. Below are some useful identifications.

LUCAS MODEL NUMBERS

PREFIXES

B – Ball bearing
D – Distributor
E – Electronic
H – Horizontal cable outlets
K – Small cast-iron body with moulded contact breaker base and die-cast advance weights
KY – Die-cast body with a pressed-steel contact-breaker plate
M – Micro-control
P – Porous bushing
U – Large cast-iron body with moulded contact-breaker base
V – Built in vacuum control
X – Hardened steel auto-advance mechanism
Y – Large cast-iron body with pressed-steel contact-breaker plate and die-cast advance weights
Z – Rolling weights advance mechanism

SUFFIXES

1 – Single cylinder
2 – Twin cylinder
4 – 4-cylinder
6 – 6-cylinder
8 – 8-cylinder
A – Auto advance or retard fitted

These made up models with numbers such as DMBZ6A, DM6 DKY4A. These were used up to the 1960s, when they changed to using models such as 25D4, 45D4, 22D6. Again, here the suffix number indicated the number of cylinders.

PART NUMBERS

Lucas distributors usually had either five- or six-figure numbers beginning with a '4'; military versions however used a different numbering system. These numbers, for example 40510, designated which car they were fitted to, and what the specification of the distributor was – that is, what the advance curve was, what cap was fitted, and what drive gear it had.

DELCO MODEL NUMBERS

Delco used a similar system of model number, such as D200, D204, determining the style of distributor, and then an individual part number, such as 7953166, determining the specification of that individual unit.

SPARK PLUGS

CHAMPION SPARK PLUGS

Prefixes First Character
B – Taper seat
C – Bantam type (short overall length)
D – Taper-seat Bantam type
E – Shielded
O – Wire-wound resistor
Q – Inductive suppressor
R – Resistor
T – Special Bantam type
U – Auxiliary gap
X – Resistor

Prefixes Second Character
A – 12mm thread, ¾in (19mm) reach
C – 14mm thread, ¾in (19mm) reach
D – 18mm thread, ½in (12.7mm) reach

F – 18mm thread, 0.460in (11.7mm) reach
G – 10mm thread, ¾in (19mm) reach
H – 14mm thread, ⁷⁄₁₆in (11.1mm) reach
J – 14mm thread, ⅜in (9.5mm) reach
K – 18mm thread, different reach
L – 14mm thread, ½in (12.7mm) or 0.472in (12mm) reach
N – 14mm thread, ¾in (19mm) reach
P – 12mm thread, 0.492in (12.5mm) reach
R – 12mm thread, ¾in (19mm) reach
S – 14mm thread, 0.708in (18mm) reach
V – 14mm thread, 0.460in (11.7mm) reach
W – ⁷⁄₈in × 18, different reach
Y – 10mm thread, ¼in (6.3mm) or ⁵⁄₁₆in (7.9mm) reach
Z – 10mm thread, 0.492in (12.5mm) reach

Number

1–25 General use
26–50 Aviation
51–75 Racing
76–379 Special features

For general spark plugs, the lower the number the colder the plug, the higher the number the hotter the plug.

Suffix

A – Conventional
B – Multiple-earth electrode
C – Copper-cored centre electrode
G – Precious-metal centre electrode
H – Projected core nose

J – Cut-back earth electrode
R – Racing-type electrode, push-in wire electrode
V – Surface gap
X – Special features
YC – Projected cone nose and copper-cored electrode
CC – Copper-cored ground electrode
GY – Projected core nose and precious-metal centre electrode
BYC – Projected core nose, copper-cored electrode and three earth electrodes

End number

4 – 1mm electrode gap
5 – 1.3mm electrode gap
6 – 1.5mm electrode gap
8 – 2mm electrode gap

NGK

The table opposite refers to the NGK numbering system

LODGE PLUGS

The first letter on a Lodge plug relates to the heat range of the plug: B, C, H.

Subsequent letters are as follows:
A – ⅜in reach
L – ¾in reach
N – Non-detachable
R – Racing
Y – Extended nose
V – Heavy duty
T – Taper seat

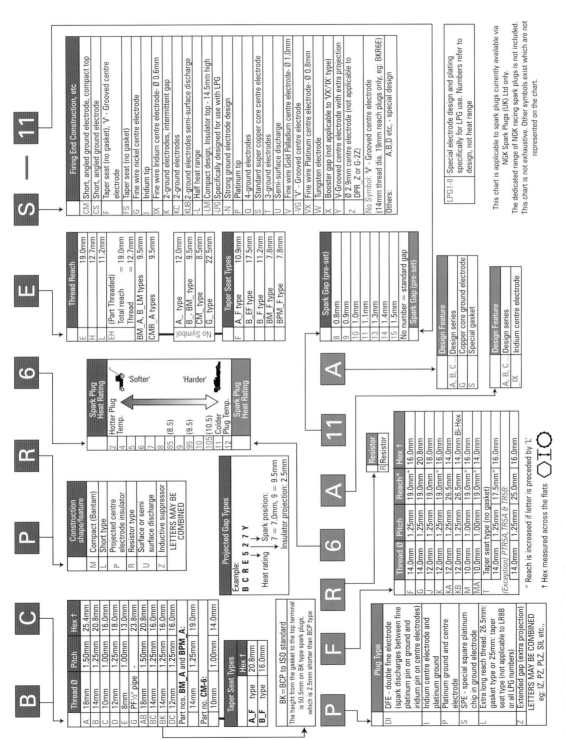

Fig. 100: NGK spark plug identification chart. NGK

SPARK PLUG CROSS-REFERENCE TABLE

The table below is given as a guide only.

CHAMPION	LODGE	KLG	NGK
L7	H14	F70, F75	B6HS
L10	CN	F50	B6H, B4H
L87Y	HNY	F85P	BP6HS, BP7H
N10Y	HLNY	FE125P, FE85P	BP6ES
N11Y	CLNY	FE55P	BP5ES
N12Y	CLNY	FE55P	BP5ES
N3	3HLN	FE100	B8ES
N5	CLN, HL, HBLN	FE75	B6ES, B5ES, B6E
N7Y	2HLNY	FE135P, FE95P	BP7ES
N8Y	HLNY	FE125P, FE85P	BP6ES
N9Y	HLNY	GT6L, FE65P	BP7E
Z10	2HL10	T90,	C6HB, C7HS
D9,D16	CV, HBV	M50,M60	A6

GLOSSARY

advance curve The amount of ignition degrees of advance in relation to the speed that the distributor is turning, throughout the whole rev range.

BTDC Before top dead centre. The amount of degrees before piston number one reaches its highest point: dead centre.

combustion chamber The space created between the top of the piston and the cylinder head. This is where the fuel mixture is ignited.

drive dog An offset drive gear fitted to the bottom of the distributor shaft and locating to the distributor drive inside the engine.

dwell angle The number of degrees of rotation of the distributor during which the points are closed.

Hall effect Magnetic electronic ignition, named after Edwin Hall who first discovered the principle on which it is based.

HT High tension.

LT Low tension.

OE Original equipment.

overlap The period in an engine when both the inlet and exhaust valves are open at the same time.

primary winding The low-tension windings of the ignition coil.

rpm Revolutions per minute. The number of complete revolutions the engine makes in one minute.

secondary winding The high-tension windings of the ignition coil.

static timing Setting the timing with the engine turned off.

TDC Top dead centre, when piston number one is at its furthest distance from the crankshaft.

USEFUL CONTACTS

Autocar Electrical Ltd
49-51 Tiverton Street, London, SE1 6NZ
0207 403 4334 www.newtronic.co.uk

Boyer-Bransden Electronics Ltd
Frindsbury House, Cox Street, Detling, Maidstone,
   Kent, ME14 3HE
01622 730939
www.boyerbransden.com

British Vacuum Unit
112 Briar Bush Rd, Canterbury, New Hampshire
   03224, USA

The Green Spark Plug Company
Mocliffe, 29 Northwich Road, Cranage, Cheshire,
   CW4 8HL
01477 532317 www.gsparkplug.com

Gunsons
The Tool Connection Ltd, Kineton Road, Southam,
   Warwickshire, CV47 0DR
01926 815000 www.gunson.co.uk

H & H Ignition Solutions
Unit H, The Wallows, Fenns Pool Avenue,
   Brierley Hill, West Midlands, DY5 1QA
01384 261500 www.h-h-ignitionsolutions.co.uk

123 Ignition
0031-182-611412
www.123ignition.nl

Magnecor Europe Limited
Unit 12, Jubilee Business Park, Snarestone Road,
   Appleby Magna, Derbyshire, DE12 7AJ
01530 274975
www.magnecor.co.uk

NGK Spark Plugs (UK) Ltd
Maylands Avenue, Hemel Hempstead,
   Hertfordshire, HP2 4SD
01442 281000
www.ngkntk.co.uk

Pertronix Europe
1 Compton Place, Surrey Avenue, Camberley,
   Surrey, GU15 3DX
01276 65554
www.pertronixeurope.com

Retro Classic Car Parts Ltd
The Old Surgery, Jay Lane, Leintwardine,
   Shropshire, SY7 0LG
01547 540800
www.retroclassiccarparts.com

Satel snc
Contrada Papagnano, 63848 Petritoli (FM), Italy
Tel/fax 0734/658720
www.electronicspark.it

INDEX